Writers of Wales

Editors
MEIC STEPHENS R. BRINLEY JONES

Gwyn Williams

AN INTRODUCTION TO WELSH LITERATURE

University of Wales Press

Cardiff 1992

I

I once heard Arnold Toynbee say that, compared to the million years or so of man's existence on this earth as *Homo sapiens*, the five thousand years of what we usually think of as civilization is so short a period in proportion that everything within it should be considered as contemporary. If Homer, as Toynbee claimed, is our contemporary, so much the more are Taliesin, Hywel ab Owain Gwynedd and Dafydd ap Gwilym, and unless we approach these writers as contemporaries, with something living to say to us today, since what they wrote and did is part of our curious amalgam of Welsh life and thought and art today, then we will do little more than pick them up, brush off a little dust, and put them down again, as one does with a friend's collection of bric-à-brac.

The earliest Welsh poetry which we have comes from the second half of the sixth century AD, the age of resistance to the Anglo-Saxon penetration of the island of Britain. We do not know for how many centuries before that poets had composed and orators had declaimed in earlier forms of Welsh. Poseidonius, writing towards the end of the second century BC, reports that the Celts called their poets *bardoi*. The modern Welsh word for poet is still *bardd*. Julius Caesar says that the Druids, whose educational centre was in Anglesey, used verses as an aid to memory, as we still do today to remember the number of days in a month. When in our museums we observe the sophistication, balance and purity of form of our ancestors' work in gold, bronze, iron and stone, their bronze hand-mirrors and gold torques, the Trawsfynydd tankard, the Capel Garmon fire-dog, we are not surprised to be told by Diodorus Siculus, who wrote in the first century BC, that when a Celtic chieftain travelled he took with him hunts-men, hounds and minstrels. A millennium later, the laws of Hywel Dda accord a place of honour to the falconer and the poet in a Welsh king's entourage.

Even without all this we may, from the sixth-century Welsh poetry, deduce a long established tradition of versifying in praise of heroes. Rhyme and other basic elements of *cynghanedd*, our complex system of interplay between vowels and consonants which is still followed, are already present in the work of Taliesin and Aneirin. In Taliesin's poem on the Battle of Argoed Llwyfain, fought in the second half of the sixth century, one catches the chiming of internal and end rhyme and the beginnings of complex alliter-ation. And occasionally, in this very early poetry with all its difficulties for the non-specialist reader, a line hits us with simple and immediate comprehensi-bility, as when Aneirin, in his heroic poem 'Gododdin', says,

> . . .*a gwedy elwch tawelwch fu.*

> (. . .*and after rejoicing there was silence.*)

Taliesin sang the praises of Urien, king of Rheged (south-western Scotland today), and his son Owain, who fought against the Angles under Hussa. Aneirin praised Mynyddog Mwynfawr, king of the Gododdin tribe, who held court at Dineidin, present-day

Edinburgh, and the group of young men who trained for a year at Mynyddog's court, called together from different parts of Celtic Britain in preparation for a kind of commando attack on the English at Catraeth, probably Catterick. The poem, known as 'Gododdin', is a sequence of passages which vividly sketch the nature and bearing of the different young heroes. Silence follows rejoicing because all, or nearly all the young men were killed, whilst inflicting much heavier casualties on the English. The poem tells us that they paid for the mead, the sweet mead of Mynyddog's hall, which thus became their poison. Payment for mead symbolizes the service which was the young man's duty in repayment for the chieftain's hospitality. So, after a year's training and feasting, the young men rode out on their spirited horses, in fine tunics and with torques of gold and good steel weapons. There is no need for us to think that they were drunk when they set out, as has been suggested, though there was no shame in having sometimes drunk too much during the year's train- ing, as the twelfth-century Owain Cyfeiliog reminds us in his recapturing of the earlier heroic age, when, in his 'Hirlas Owain', he calls on the bearer of the mead horn to pour from the horn for Cynfelyn, 'honourably drunk on foaming mead'.

Yes, these early Welsh poems were composed in Scotland, at a time when the language spoken there was the Early Welsh which had then recently envolved by phonetic change from the earlier Brittonic form of Celtic. A common language and a common culture linked what was to become Cymru with northern Britain, until the seventh-century drive of the Anglo-Saxons separated the two regions. There may already have been a movement of people and tradition from the North to north Wales before the Scotti came over from northern Ireland and the Celtic nations settled down to the geographical areas they inhabit today. Tradition associates this movement with the name of Cunedda and his sons. During the centuries of Roman occupation there had been invasions from Ireland into north and south Wales. Cunedda is said to have driven the Irish out of north Wales in the early years of the fifth century, but the Irish influence in south Wales was stronger and more lasting. In Llandudoch (St Dogmaels) Church, near Cardigan, there is an interesting bilingual memorial stone of the fifth or sixth century. The scripts employed are Latin and Ogham, the Irish alphabet which ran along the spine of the trimmed edge of the stone, and the equivalent of the Latin *fili* is not the Welsh *mab* or *ap* (son of) but the Irish *maqi*. These ogham stones are mostly to be found in south Wales, where Irish influence is to be observed in sculpture, mythology and language, and it is possible that, but for the drive from north Wales, Goidelic and eventually a language like modern Irish might have become the language of south Wales.

Welsh poetry, from the seventh century on, was to be composed in Wales, except for the nostalgic utterances of those who ventured abroad from their homeland. The earliest Welsh poetry has been preserved for us chiefly in four famous manuscripts, the Black Book of Carmarthen (mid-thirteenth century), the Book of Aneirin (*c*. 1250), the Book of Taliesin (written probably in mid or south Wales *c*. 1300–25) and the Red Book of Hergest (*c*. 1400). In addition to the earliest poetry, these manuscripts also contain other poems written from the seventh century to the date of the writing of the manuscripts,

4

poems that indicate that the function of the poet was not confined to the singing of the praise of his chieftain or patron. Interpolated into the warlike Book of Aneirin is a lovely song sung by a mother to her little son, Dinogad. From the ninth century is a poem in praise of Tenby in the Book of Taliesin, a poem which gives a stirring picture of poets and warriors carousing together in the safety of a fortress. 'Llyfr Du Caerfyrddin' (the Black Book of Carmarthen) has difficult prophetic poems attributed to a sixth-century Myrddin who became the Merlin of Arthurian legend. Some of these poems may have sixth-century material, others are clearly pastiches of the old manner to fit twelfth- and thirteenth-century situations. Professor Geraint Gruffydd has suggested that the prestige of vaticination, or prophetic writing, best exemplified in the attitude towards the perhaps mythical Myrddin and his verse, is the ancient source of the especial esteem and awe in which poets have been held in the Celtic world. They were believed to be in touch with forces outside our everyday concerns. Satire and cursing poetry are an aspect of this supernatural power and the disapproval expressed by the medieval church for this kind of writing is a recognition of its power. We have fierce enough poems in Welsh, but modern Welsh poetry has no such frightening examples of cursing poetry as we find in the work of James Stephens and J. M. Synge.

The Black Book has some of our earliest religious poetry, as well as a fascinating sequence known as 'Englynion y Beddau' (*Stanzas of the Graves*) which record the burial places of men and women, most of whom are merely names to us, so far do they take us back into mythology and to ages before recorded history. They are buried not usually in churchyards

5

but in moorland or on sea strand remote from human habitation, and the long sequence begins with the line,

Y beddau a'u gwlych y glaw. . .

(The graves that the rain wets. . .)

The mystery of Arthur's grave is referred to, but may some of these stanzas belong to the Bronze Age four-square graves of our hilltops? One such grave is described in the stanzas. Impressive, and perhaps an argument in favour of the great antiquity of the stanzas, is the fact that the monkish scribes of Caerfyrddin made no attempt to set one at least of these famous graves within their own precincts, a medieval practice which Joseph Bédier unmasked in his LES LÉGENDES EPIQUES.

Much of our earliest poetry was, by the time it was written down, of unknown authorship, but tradition, enshrined in the *Historia Brittonum* attributed to Nennius (written 829–30), gives us the names of famous poets, Talhaearn, Bluchbard and Cian, none of whose poems have survived. Talhaearn is called 'Tad Awen' (*Father of the Muse*) and we regret the disappearance of his work, or perhaps one should say our inability to ascribe any of the anonymous verse to him.

Many of the shorter poems we have from this early period are interpolations, like the Dinogad song, into unrelated contexts. Thus twelve stanzas in an old *englyn* form were written, probably early in the tenth century, into the margin of the Juvencus Manuscript, a Latin paraphrase of the Gospels, with Welsh

6

glosses, now in the Cambridge University library. Nine of these are religious and frightfully difficult to understand, but the other three, made comprehensible for us by the interpretation of Sir Ifor Williams, tell of the gloom of a warrior with a sadly reduced retinue, just one foreign mercenary, benighted after a disastrous raid or battle. The heroic age was not all feasting, successful raids and correct behaviour between bard and patron. There was holocaust, gloom and death. But by the happy chance of manuscript survival almost every aspect of life in those days is recorded for us in the poetry we have, with the exception of love between man and woman. It is said of one young man, in the second stanza of 'Y Gododdin',

> *Diademed and to the fore wherever he came,*
> *breathless before a girl, he paid for his mead.*

That is all. Sexual love was not then a subject for poetry, certainly not poetry worthy of recording. For that we must wait until the second heroic age of twelfth-century Wales and then spasmodically with the swing of taste, or religion and the character of individual poets, in the ages that followed.

II

Defeat in battle had broken the land links between the Celtic parts of Britain and late in the eighth century a mutually agreed wall, known as Offa's Dyke, after the Mercian king who planned it, separated Wales and England. But there was no permanent peace, especially in the border country, and it is from poetry that we learn most about the wars and raids between Powys and Mercia. From those bitter days probably sprang the English rhyme 'Taffy was a Welshman' and its record of a cattle raid, the driving back of cattle on the hoof, 'a leg of beef', the subsequent retaliation and the burning of a Welsh homestead. The poems associated with the old chieftain Llywarch Hen, and with the noble girl Heledd, sketch for us a grim picture of these conflicts. These poems have been interpreted by Sir Ifor Williams as the verse high-spots in prose sagas about these historical sixth- and seventh-century figures, the verse interpolations perhaps preserved as memory aids for the teller of the story and then, as verse, recorded in manuscript as the tale faded into oblivion. In the form in which we have them, these poems are thought to belong to the ninth century. They are classed as anonymous, but so intensely personal is the note in these Llywarch and Heledd poems that it is with reluctance that I give up Llywarch the poet and Heledd as our first woman poet. Surviving out of this presumed saga context the poems however stand splendidly on their own.

The Llywarch series is a notable statement on war and peace, and in lamenting the death of Gwên, the last of his twenty-four sons, he says,

Through my tongue they were killed. . .

for it was he who inspired and urged on their wars with the English. The famous lament for his old age sums up the deprivations and humiliations of senility.

The laments of Heledd are even more poignant and are unmistakably feminine. Her brother Cynddylan has been killed in battle and his hall at Pengwern, possibly at or near present-day Shrewsbury, is in flames, whilst the eagle tears at his body. This is heart-rending poetry but brilliantly clear and unsentimental in its language and imagery. The Heledd and Llywarch poems were gathered together in the Red Book of Hergest.

A poem from the Black Book of Carmarthen, entitled 'Gereint Filius Erbin', gives us a glimpse of Arthur in the fierce onrush of mounted warfare, as well as our first and grimmest view in literature of the future Geraint of romance.

From these bitter centuries also comes a body of gnomic and nature poetry, poems about the weather and its effects which incorporate traditional wisdom, often in the last line of a stanza. These are statements which were already or have since become proverbs, perhaps the relics of the ancient shamanist or druidic functions of the poet, and his wisdom is sometimes put into the mouths of birds and beasts.

*Did you hear what the fish sang
as he floundered among the stalks?
Nature is stronger than education.*

Sometimes, within the framework of the countryside's changing moods and seasons, and the
enshrining of common sense, we are given glimpses
of individual human misery, like the despair of a
leper, comparable to that of Llywarch and Heledd.
This varied lyrical, rather than heroic, verse has been
edited by Sir Ifor Williams, mostly from the Black
Book and the Red Book of Hergest under the title
CANU LLYWARCH HEN.

Prophetic poetry, involving satire and political
propaganda, continued to be written so long as the
wars went on, and the long 'Armes Prydain' from
the Book of Taliesin refers so closely to the happenings of its day that is has been possible to assign it to
about the year 930.

I have already linked an ancient Celtic respect for the
poet with the laws of Hywel Dda. Though we have
no proofs that these laws existed in written form
before the twelfth century, the traditions are strong
that early in the tenth century this king, who had
succeeded in uniting most of Wales under his control, codified existing Welsh law and caused manuscript copies to be made. These extraordinary
detailed laws, setting forth the rights of every man,
woman and child, the redress for every wrong and
the value of every useful thing if stolen or malicious-
ly destroyed, are worded in clear, powerful and
occasionally blunt Welsh. Though the villein, tied as
he was to the land he worked on for some petty
king, or large or small landowner, was not allowed

to acquire or practise the superior crafts of black-smith or poet, he too had his rights and was protected in his station. The grades of bard are laid down and the nature and number of poems expected from retinue poet or king's poet, as well as the rights and pickings he may expect from his post, are all part of the law.

These laws, as I have suggested, are in a prose that was meant to be understood, and they were probably modified to the requirements of each age, at least up to 1282. One of the legal duties of a court poet was not only to sing of royalty but of God, and the Black Book of Carmarthen, as befits a manuscript put together in a religious foundation, has examples of such poetry. There you will find a poem which begins,

> *Moli Duw yn nechrau a diwedd*
>
> *(To praise God at beginning and end),*

whilst in another, which begins,

> *Gogonedawg arglwydd henffych well*
>
> *(Glorious lord all hail)*

God is glorified not only by church and chancel, men and women, but by all aspects of nature, the earth and the stars.

III

Reference has already been made to prose tales in which short passages of verse, which we now accept as lyrics in their own right, were possibly embedded. Whoever composed these tales, the entertainer who recited them to whatever audience he could find was known as *cyfarwydd*. In modern Welsh the word *cyfarwydd* has degenerated to the feebler meaning of familiar, in the sense of being familiar with, but in medieval Welsh it meant not only one with a repertoire of tales but an expert in other fields, including that of magic. It is against the background of traditional expertise in story-telling that we place the artistry of 'Pedair Cainc y Mabinogi' (*The Four Branches of the Mabinogi*). In the story of *Math* we are told that Gwydion was the greatest *cyfarwydd* in the world, and Gwydion was a Celtic god, whose *caer* or fortress is the Milky Way. Scholarship has indicated that these tales were put together in the form we have them some time in the late eleventh or early twelfth century, but there has been much argument, argument which will surely never be resolved, about their ultimate age. Without doubting the basic antiquity of the tales, material that goes back to myth and primitive religion, material which already existed in sometimes conflicting versions, Saunders Lewis has pointed out similarities between them and the relationship between Gwynedd, Deheubarth and Henry II, the chivalric elements and the echoes of Geoffrey of Monmouth's HISTORIA REGUM BRITANNIAE, all these leading him to believe that quite late in the twelfth century is the time when these tales were given their final form. There is much more than stuff for recital by a *cyfarwydd* here, he claims. These tales are the written work of a conscious literary artist who took the opportunity to introduce contemporary parallels which would be seized upon by the more knowing of his audience. Saunders Lewis proposes a monk at Strata Florida Abbey in the last twenty years of the twelfth century as the one author of *The Four Branches*. Some scholars assert that there was one author of these four tales, a master of language who selected from and fused this material into triumphs of prose writing, while others favour multiple authorship.

The word *mabinogi* may have meant a tale of the youth of a hero, being extended to include his later exploits and his death, with a wealth of incident concerning other persons in his story. Eric Hamp, however, has suggested that it originally designated material relating to the god Mabon. W. J. Gruffydd proposed Pryderi as the central figure of *The Four Branches*, which in turn deal with the birth, imprisonment, adventures and death of this legendary hero of south-western Dyfed. The strangeness of the tales, surely evidence of great antiquity, lies in the close co-existence of the normal world and Annwn, the underworld, which is established in the opening lines of the *mabinogi* of 'Pwyll, Chieftain of Dyfed'. Pwyll one day left Arberth, present-day Narberth, to hunt in Glyn Cuch with his retinue and his dogs. There he met another horseman with a pack of strangely coloured hounds. This was Arawn, king of Annwn. They fell into friendly conversation, and Pwyll promised to take Arawn's place and appearance as king of the underworld, whilst Arawn would take his place in Dyfed. The behaviour of each ruler during the year of their exchange, Arawn's wise governing of Dyfed, Pwyll's resistance to the temptation of Arawn's bed and his performance of a promised killing, all this cemented a friendship between them and established a nearness between their two worlds. This nearness was to impinge upon later developments of the story. The tales are full of love, friendship, treachery and violence, involving links between Gwynedd, Dyfed, Ireland, Cornwall and London, where the head of Bendigeidfran, killed in Ireland, was taken to be buried in the White Hill. After the death of Pryderi in the fourth tale we are given the story of the murderous adultery and fearful punishment of Blodeuwedd. One asks whether she behaved in this way because she was made by Gwydion, with magnificent thoughtlessness, out of flowers and therefore without sense of human responsibilities, or whether this is another fore-doomed, disastrous love, like that of Trystan and Esyllt.

Associated with *The Four Branches* under the general title of THE MABINOGION, since Lady Charlotte Guest's translation, have been seven other prose tales, of later date and varying authorship and style. The two stories 'Lludd and Llefelys' and 'The Dream of Macsen Wledig' give us a folk view of the history of Britain in pre-Roman and Roman times. Lludd is said to have built the walls of Celtic London and is still remembered in Ludgate. Macsen is Magnus Maximus, rebelliously declared emperor in Britain towards the end of the fourth century, and his story not only has love for a dream girl but an explanation of how Brittany came to be settled. 'Culhwch and Olwen' is the earliest Arthurian story in European literature and the Arthur presented is forthright and Welsh, untouched as yet by Norman-French or continental sophistication. Culhwch sets off for Arthur's court to enlist help in the tasks he has to perform to win the daughter of the giant Ysbaddaden, Olwen, a golden blonde, in whose track white flowers spring as she walks along. (Her name means white track.) The account is detailed, lively and long, but the end comes suddenly and tersely. Ysbaddaden is shaved by Cadw, his head is cut off by Goreu and that night Culhwch sleeps with Olwen, who remains his only love. In 'The Dream of Rhonabwy' a young man of that name, living in the Powys of the early twelfth century, falls asleep in a hall that has seen better days and dreams of other heroic ages, those of Arthur and Owain ap Urien. The interweaving of the colourful and not quite rationally linked elements in the dream reminds one of the nature of Celtic design, as we have it on stone, metal and parchment. At the same time we sense a wry, satirical attitude on the part of the unknown author towards both heroism and the practice of poetry. We are told in a note at the end of the unique version of the tale in the Red Book of Hergest that, because of its complexity and especially the number of colours — many of them rare, used to describe horses, trappings, garments and jewels — this was not a tale of the repertoire of the reciting *cyfarwydd* but one to be read from a book.

To make up the eleven tales, first put together for translation by Lady Guest, come the three romances, 'Owein' or 'The Lady of the Fountain', 'Peredur Son of Efrawg' and 'Gereint Son of Erbin'.

The first words of 'The Lady of the Fountain' assert

a new background for this kind of writing. Arthur is now an emperor, reclining on a couch of brightly coloured brocaded silk, whilst his wife sits with her handmaidens sewing at a window. We are in a land of strange castles, mysterious woods, the chivalric concerns of jousting and the winning of a wife, of young men who set off on quests from Arthur's court. The evolution of matter and manner has been a two-way exchange. The stories are basically north British and Welsh (may not Brocéliande have been *bro Celidon*, the region of Caledonia?) and the names of people and places in them are Celtic. Through contacts with Brittany and later through the Norman-French conquerors these stories passed over to the continent and, in the course of time, awareness of the continental developments of Arthurian legend came back to Wales, once more through the Norman-French penetration of our land and culture.

Romance comes from Romanitas, the Romanized Celtic world, and chivalry sprang from a Celtic attitude towards women. The very word chivalry comes from a Roman borrowing from Celtic, for though Latin had a perfectly good word for horse, *equus*, the Roman soldiers were so impressed by the Celtic use of horses in war and travel that they took over the word *caballus* (modern Welsh *ceffyl*). The Celtic horseman was for them a *cabellarius*, as were the young men of the 'Gododdin' and Arthur and his band, and this late Latin word touched off a host of associated words in Portuguese, Spanish, French and English. Thus the Celtic world made this incalculable double contribution to the languages, literature and ethos of Europe.

IV

Resistance, often successful, to the Norman and later
Anglo-Norman penetration, particularly in Gwynedd,
gave rise to the sensation of a new heroic age. Once
more were leaders praised for their hospitality and
prowess in raid and battle. The twelfth-century
prince, Owain Cyfeiliog, composed with the
'Gododdin' in his mind in the only poem of his that
has survived. In a feast after a battle the warriors
are praised as the mead-bearer carries the great
mead-horn to each in turn, until he reaches the
empty place at the table of one who has been killed
that day. (The thirteenth-century Dafydd Benfras felt
himself to be singing in the same ancient tradition
when he began an ode to Llywelyn the Great with a
wish for

> . . .as complete a muse as the ardour of Myrddin,
> to sing praise like Aneirin did once
> the day he sang Gododdin.)

The great poets of this age seemed to take a personal
delight in the violence, the blood and the destruction
of war, perhaps because they were warriors as well
as bards. But the twelfth century offers other
elements which are new to Welsh poetry.

In 1081 Gruffudd ap Cynan came from Ireland and
by force of arms established his inherited right to the
throne of Gwynedd. His father, an exile from internecine Welsh warfare to the Viking city of Dublin,
had married the granddaughter of a Viking king of

Dublin and Gruffudd had been brought up as a Viking as well as a Welshman, and at the same time in awareness of Irish poetry and song. He is said to have brought minstrels over with him, in the accepted Celtic manner, and there is a strong tradition, though no historical evidence, that he brought about changes in the crafts of poetry and music. Was his influence therefore responsible for the new delight in love and nature which the twelfth-century poets wove into their glorification of war? Gruffudd's chief poet was Meilyr Brydydd, Meilyr the Poet, who echoes the sixth-century Taliesin in his praise of his patron, but whose most famous poem is his death-bed plea for burial amongst the saints on the island of Enlli (Bardsey).

The new elements I have mentioned are to be found in a poem by Meilyr's son Gwalchmai, who inherited his father's place at the court of Gwynedd, a poem of personal boasting called 'Gorhoffedd' (*Exultation*), but they are most beautifully expressed in the 'Gorhoffedd' and seven short odes of Hywel ab Owain Gwynedd, son of the great Owain by an Irish woman, and grandson of Gruffudd ap Cynan. Hywel ab Owain Gwynedd is the first poet in Welsh to make landscape an essential element in his delight in life.

> *I love its strand and its mountains,*
> *its castle near the woods and its fine lands,*
> *its water-meadows and its valleys,*
> *its white gulls and its lovely women. . .*
> *I love the seacoast of Meirionnydd,*
> *where a white arm was my pillow.*

Hywel ab Owain's princely status made him more

free than were the professional poets to write as he pleased, and we treasure every line he wrote about his many loves. More formal poetry to women, closer to the *amour courtois* tradition of France, was composed by other poets of this age, notably Cynddelw and Prydydd y Moch.

From Aneirin to Dafydd Benfras, in spite of the gloom of the ninth century and the happy innovations of the twelfth, there had been little change in the relationship between poet and patron, but the change was soon to come. These official, and often chieftainly, poets of the early twelfth to the early fourteenth century were, about the year 1756, given the title *Gogynfeirdd* by Lewis Morris. The term means 'not so early poets' and is intended to distinguish them and their work from Taliesin, Aneirin and the unknown authors of pre-Norman days. In English they are usually called the court poets of the princes. When Llywelyn ap Gruffudd was killed in 1282, and Edward I showed his severed head on a pike in London, these princes lost their power and their poets lost their ancient rights. In his long elegy on the death of Llywelyn, Gruffudd ab yr Ynad Coch sounds the knell of a period, of a way of living and a way of writing. As in Shakespeare's KING LEAR, all nature, the universe itself seems to be involved in this fearful fall. There is no more agonized, though controlled, cry than this in the literature of Europe.

> . . .*Don't you see that the world is in danger?*
> *A sigh to you, God, that the sea may come over the land!*
> *Why are we left to linger?*
> *There's no retreat from the prison of fear,*
> *there's nowhere to dwell, alas for the dwelling!*
> *There is no counsel, no lock, no opening,*
> *no way of delivery from terror's sad precept.*

V

In the dispirited Wales of the first half of the fourteenth century there came changes in the nature of
the poetry composed. There were no longer princes
to give top jobs to the most gifted poets, and since
there were no wars, internecine or national, patrons
could hardly be praised for their prowess in battle,
unless this was displayed in the English army, on
behalf of the English king. There seemed to be little
justification for prophetic poetry of the flattering
kind, but hospitality, especially when extended to
poets, could still provide a reason for writing in a
traditional manner. The towns established by the
Normans in the shadow of their bigger castles, towns
where the Welsh were not welcome unless as useful
craftsmen prepared to accept subservient situations,
became more prosperous and more remote from the
traditional things of Welsh life. Gruffudd ab Adda, in
a poem to a birch-tree which had been cut down to
provide a maypole for the townspeople of Llanidloes,
shows contempt for town-dwellers and their petty
commerce, offering instead the beauty of the green
woods and hills. Dafydd ap Gwilym, born in a
narrow upland valley east of Aberystwyth, took a
special, and surely revengeful, pleasure in a love
affair with Elen, wife of Robert le Northern, a
wealthy wool merchant of that town. In other poems
of his we get the feeling that for him a visit to a
town was a venture into foreign country. At the
same time, since his grandfather had held land from
the king in the lower Teifi valley and his uncle was

constable of Castellnewydd Emlyn Castle, he was probably more at home in the atmosphere of a Norman castle, where he may well have learnt about poetic happenings on the continent and been influenced by them.

Dafydd ap Gwilym came of a landed family and, like Hywel ab Owain Gwynedd, could afford to write as he pleased, not bound by what was traditionally, and at one time legally, required of the professional cadres of poets. Yet it must be stressed that he did compose poems of praise to patrons and of thanks for hospitality, and that sometimes in the stricter metres of the highest class of professional poet, though even here with a difference. Dafydd's poems of praise, of thanks or of grief at a death show us not a poet excercising his craft for payment but a man among equals, writing about friends whom he visits and whose death leaves a gap. The generous Ifor Hael has been called Dafydd's patron, but as we read Dafydd's account of life at Basaleg in Gwent, the hunting together, the indoor games, the shared delight in poetry, the buckskin gloves that Ifor gives him, it becomes clear that the relationship is one of loving friends.

> *Mawrserch Ifor a'm goryw,*
> *mwy no serch ar ordderch yw.*

(Great love of Ifor compels me, / greater than love for a loose girl.)

But many of Dafydd's poems were written to both loose and unwilling girls, as well as to his more permanent loves, the willing Morfudd and the unattainable Dyddgu. What did they mean to Dafydd, all these women, for he was clearly more than a persistent fornicator? Out of voluntary and involuntary personal and social relationships we all of us have to evolve a framework which helps us to live a decent and fairly satisfying life, compensating along certain lines for other relationships which are either not granted us or are feebly represented in our personal pattern. In the despair after 1282 Dafydd could despise the English but could take no pride in his own nation. In his poems we find no reference to mother, father, brother or sister and, so far as we know, he was never married, except for his bardic wedding with Morfudd conducted by Madog Benfras in the woods. And there is no record that he had any acknowledged children. This apparent deprivation, whether by chance or choice, narrowed the links with his fellow humans down to friendship, with fellow poets and with men like Ifor Hael, the friendship of women, too, and the love of women. On the evidence of his poems, love was for him most happily an outdoor activity of early summer, a shared rite of spring set in the reborn green wood, giving him a mystical sense of entering into the rhythm of the universe. This experience was so important to him that he sometimes uses the lovely terms of the Catholic faith in Welsh to express it, for though Dafydd clearly accepted that faith, I cannot see that it gave him an important element in the framework he needed. It can, of course, be argued that he took nature to be a revelation of the glory of God, and a poem translated as 'The Woodland Mass' and beginning with the words *Lle digrif y bum heddiw*, can be interpreted either way. He is listening at dawn to a cock thrush singing.

> Then the slim eloquent nightingale
> from the corner of a grove nearby,
> poetess of the valley, sings to the many
> the Sanctus bell in lively whistling.
> The sacrifice is raised
> up to the sky above the bush,
> devotion to God the Father,
> the chalice of ecstasy and love.
> The psalmody contents me;
> it was bred of a birch-grove in the sweet woods.

To such a setting he invites his loves, for the birch-grove is sacred to love. The laughable, comical experiences generally occur indoors; the desperate trouble he got into on his way to a girl's bed at an inn; his escape from an irate husband into a goose shed; the girl at another inn who poured his offered wine over his page's head; the mockery he suffered from the Llanbadarn girls whom he went to church to ogle. All this he reports because he possesses the rare faculty of being able to laugh at himself. It isn't always springtime, and Dafydd often found nature in a discouraging mood. He tells us of the wave that swept up from the sea when he was wading across the River Dyfi to see Morfudd; of the mist that led him astray on his way to meet another girl; of the rain dripping down on him from the eaves whilst he hopes to be let in; and even a bright night which allowed a jealous husband to spot him as he lurked outside the house.

We are lucky to have such a considerable body of indubitable work by Dafydd ap Gwilym, about one hundred and forty *cywyddau* as well as many *englynion* and poems in other *awdl* metres. The immense scholarship of Dr Thomas Parry in GWAITH

23

DAFYDD AP GWILYM has gone far towards establishing a definitive canon of his work.

Of his mastery of language and of the craft of Welsh versification, of the ease with which he acclimatized foreign words in the Welsh language, of the untranslatable beauty of his writing it is difficult to write without lengthy quotation from the original poetry. Dafydd ap Gwilym is our most varied, our livelist, our greatest poet. Most of his work is in the *cywydd deuair hirion* form, a form which he seems to have popularized and which has been much used since his day. Such a poem is rarely less than fifteen or more than one hundred lines in length. It consists of seven-syllable couplets, a stressed syllable always rhyming with an unstressed one, with any of the devices of *cynghanedd* liberally employed.

It was not only his freedom as a non-professional but the chaos into which the practice of poetry had fallen that enabled Dafydd ap Gwilym to use this *cywydd* for such serious, top-grade purposes as praise or mourning. The old relationship between teacher and pupil in the craft of verse had slackened and the *clerwr*, the *jongleur* or lower grade of poetic entertainer, whose verse was often satirical, bawdy and careless of the strict measures, had insinuated himself from inn and market place to gentleman's hall and monastery refectory. Saunders Lewis has pointed out that a reform of the Cistercian monasteries was ordered in 1335 and that this went together with a re-affirmation of the grades of Welsh poet. In this century, too, the teachers of the craft of writing became seriously worried by the temporary lack of respect for the old metres and for correctness in writing. So they produced textbooks of composition which they called *gramadegau* or grammar books, different from our modern grammars in that they offered a philosophical or logical view of language and gave detailed instruction in verse form. The earliest names associated with these grammars are those of Einion Offeiriad and Dafydd Ddu. Such treatises continued to be written up to the sixteenth century, amongst others by such poets as Dafydd ab Edmwnd and Simwnt Fychan. In such a grammar in the Red Book of Hergest there is a list of triads, an old Welsh device to aid the student's or the *cyfarwydd*'s memory. Three things a good poet must not do are to drink too much, to womanize and to behave like a *clerwr*. Three parts of his duty are to praise, to entertain and to avoid satirical or defamatory verse. A treatise in MS Peniarth 20 offers what Saunders Lewis considers the best prose in this kind of writing.

The freedom of the new *cywydd* enabled Gruffudd Gryg to give the yew tree over Dafydd ap Gwilym's grave at Strata Florida, *ger mur Ystrad Fflur a'i phlas*, the immortality of the poet himself, and the tree is still there today. Gruffudd Gryg sees out the fourteenth century with a poem in the Dafydd manner, addressed to the moon, in which he heaps up comparisons and references, the technique known as *dyfalu*, in a plea to the cold-faced, stormy moon of April to give way to the friendlier moon of May. His reason is not, as it would be for Dafydd, to see the return of the season of loving; the poem makes it clear that Gruffudd Gryg fears for his life in a possible shipwreck on his way home from a pilgrimage to St James of Compostella. This is one of the few sea poems in Welsh, for the Welsh poets, unlike the Celtic saints, have rarely ventured far over water.

VI

Welsh scholars and critics have paid much more attention to poetry than to the other craft of words. Yet at one time the *cyfarwydd* or tale teller may have been as respected as the poet, and perhaps more eagerly listened to. One fails to find a reference to the *cyfarwydd* and his place in society in the old Welsh laws, so it has been suggested that the telling of old tales was once one of the functions of the poet, with audiences to fit the grade he had achieved, from the king's hall to the market-place. When, in the twelfth century, scribes, mostly monkish, began to put into writing the known literature of the earlier centuries, the tendency may have been to record any verse elements in a tale and to let the prose background to the tale fade from the collective memory. Obviously the tale was never quite the same, even when recited again by the same *cyfarwydd*, new emphases and up-to-date modifications would be observed by those seriously interested in literature, who might therefore not think it proper to catch the tale and fix it in manuscript at any one point in its development. Exceptions are of course the stories known as THE MABINOGION, where conscious artists in prose achieved such a splendid rewriting that it was accepted as definitive and so recorded. Until this was done and even when this was done, the native Welsh tales were not ascribed to any individual authors.

It is sad to think of the hundreds of tales of gods and heroes that have vanished for ever. We get some idea of the number of them from the old triads known as *Trioedd Ynys Prydain*, which give groups in threes of story headings classified into themes. Thus the counterpart of the Three Faithful Retinues of the Island of Britain is the Three Disloyal Retinues. For each of the six examples there must once have been a fully detailed tale. The triads were probably a memory aid and a handy repertoire for an audience to choose from. For us they are a tatalizing memorial of what we have lost.

Some of the oldest manuscripts were little libraries in themselves. It became the custom for a cultured gentleman to commission a copyist, usually a monk, to make a collection of reading matter for himself and his family. 'Llyfr Ancr Llanddewibrefi' (the Book of the Anchorite of Llanddewibrefi) was such a collection, and Sir Idris Foster has shown that the learned recluse of unknown name was the collector and copier, not the translator of the works in the manuscript. For this was a great age of translation into Welsh. Latin was not only the language of the church in Wales, it was the international language of European scholarship and by translation, mostly from Latin, knowledge of the great books and ideas of early medieval Europe came to Wales, some of these ideas in a tradition which went back to Plato and Aristotle.

The Llanddewibrefi anchorite's great collection has passages translated from the Bible, the Ten Commandments, the Lord's Prayer and the *In principio* verses from the beginning of the St John Gospel, which start in the Welsh of 1346 with the words,

Yn y dechreu yr oed geir. Ar geir a oed gyt a duw. A duw oed y geir.

It has a version of the *Elucidarium* (Iolo Goch's 'Lusudarius'), which deals with the Catholic faith in the form of catechism. Then there's the story of Prester John, known in Welsh as Ieuan Fendigaid, and lives of St David and St Beuno, and an incomplete but beautifully written treatise on the holy life, 'Kyssegyrlan Uuched'. Other similar collections have more lives of saints, many of which were originally written in Latin, though by Welshmen. Many of the earliest lives are of women saints, Catherine, Margaret, Mary Magdalen, Martha, Mary of Egypt, Ursula. Professor Caerwyn Williams tells us that the medieval reader gained as much pleasure from a saintly biography as a *chanson de geste*, and many of them are still very good reading.

We get some lively stories about Charlemagne and his knights, including 'Pererindod Siarlymaen'in the Red Book of Hergest, a Welsh prose version of the thirteenth-century Pèlerinage DE Charlemagne, which recounts the fantastic but unhistorical exploits of the emperor in Jerusalem and Constantinople.

There are historical texts too, a history of Gruffudd ap Cynan, in the thirteenth-century MS Peniarth 17, which Professor Simon Evans suggests was written first in Latin for international reading, as both an apologia for the great leader and propaganda for his son, Owain Gwynedd. *Brut Dingestow* is a Welsh version of Geoffrey of Monmouth's Historia Regum Britanniae. In the White Book of Rhydderch, written *c.* 1350, there are some apt remarks on the problems of translating made by one Gruffudd Bola, translator of the Athanasian Creed.

One forms some idea of the kind of training a young Welsh poet received in the Middle Ages from what are known as *areithiau* scattered through the manuscripts. (Some have been selected and edited by Gwenallt Jones in YR AREITHIAU PROS.) *Araith* means speech, and the word was used in the grammars for the Latin term *oratio*. The young aspirant was set an exercise, to compose a speech of loved things, of hated things, of asking, of satire or parody, of love or of grammar itself, often pretending that he is speaking for someone like Dafydd ap Gwilym or Owain Cyfeiliog. The purpose was to heap up epithets, employing compound words, to widen the writer's vocabulary and to provide him with a stock of fine-sounding descriptive words. This prentice work can be amusing to read and offers very extraordinary prose.

VII

Not all the poets made use of the new freedom to ignore the strictures of the master-teachers and to write *cywyddau* about the beauty of the world and the beauty of woman, as did Dafydd ap Gwilym, Madog, Benfras, Sypyn Cyfeiliog and Gruffudd ap Adda. As the fourteenth century progressed, some landowners returned to the old traditions and gave the better poets a place of honour in their halls. Gruffudd ap Maredudd, poet and landowner in Anglesey, thought little of the *cywydd* and all this writing about nature. He used the old *awdl* metres to write in the twelfth-century manner of love and courage. A remarkable prophetic *awdl* of his in the Red Book of Hergest calls on Owain Lawgoch to come from France to win back freedom for Wales. This, of course, was before the English contrived the murder of that renowned soldier in France. This difficult poem thunders bloodthirstily along rather in the style of Cynddelw.

> . . .*Kyrch Lundein Ywein awydd Elffin:*
> *kerdda oddyna dinas Edwin.*
> *Gwna varglwydd gwawtlwydd gwaetlin gwyarwlych*
> *a gwedy delych gwaet hyt deulin.*

Iolo Goch, a master poet of the second half of the fourteenth century, used the *cywydd* form to cover the whole range of subject matter, from the beauty of girls to poems in honour of St Anne, St David and the Twelve Apostles.

A poem which may show awareness of contemporary peasant discontent is one to the farm labourer or ploughman, but following the ancient tradition he takes the praise of patrons to be one of his main functions, and he likes his patrons to acknowledge his own rights. He describes his reception at the bishop's palace at Llanelwy (St Asaph) and its recognition of his status.

> . . .*I am caused to be placed*
> *correctly in this hall,*
> *to sit, when silence is proclaimed,*
> *fine custom, at high table. . .*
> *Drink for drink comes to me*
> *from his vineyard, from his fair hand,*
> *and poetry, eloquent of longing,*
> *and music; we get glory.*
> *A fair sweet quiet concert,*
> *then pipes and dancing every day. . .*

No poet has ever appreciated good food, good wine and civilized entertainment more than Iolo did.

Iolo wrote in praise of Owain Glyndŵr and versified his family tree, but did not live to see his rebellion. He found it possible to praise Edward III in verse and there is a *gogynfeirdd* taste for violence in his *cywydd* to Sir Hywel of the Axe, who performed prodigies in the English wars in France. But he could also joke about himself, for he writes about his unshaven beard scratching a girl's face, as Dafydd ap Gwilym had done, the Dafydd whom Iolo calls *hebog merched Deheubarth*, the hawk of the girls of the South, in an elegy he wrote on Dafydd's death. Iolo Goch is a great poet and his work admirably sums up the lines of development of Welsh poetry towards the end of the fourteenth century.

Iolo also wrote an elegy on the death of Llywelyn Goch ap Meurig Hen, whom the Welsh dictionary of biography (Y BYWGRAFFIADUR CYMREIG) gives as one of the last of the *Gogynfeirdd*. He certainly used the stricter *awdl* metres to praise God and the nobility, but he is most famous for a *cywydd* on the death of Lleucu Llwyd, wife of one Dafydd Ddu (whether the author of the famous grammar I do not know, but the date is right). Nor do we know whether she was his mistress or whether this lovely poem is a piece of *amour courtois* writing for a friend or patron, but it incorporates an astonishing innovation, an *aubade* to a dead woman who sleeps too long in her earth-bed. Llywelyn Goch was an aristocrat and free to compose as he wished.

The fifteenth century is often called the great century, not because it produced any better poets than Dafydd ap Gwilym and Iolo Goch but because of the extraordinary number of good poets that it gave light to. Many of the poems of the first half of this century are by unknown poets or are of uncertain attribution. What amazes one in reading Welsh verse of the fifteenth century is the variety of interest and experience expressed, the consistent skill in handling the *cywydd* form, the freshness, clarity and power of the language, the sustained delight, with one notable exception, in our life in this world.

Owain Glyndŵr's rebellion, with its brief translation into fact of the dream of a self-governing Wales, and his civilized plans for the country, all this had faded with the declining fortunes of the leader. We do not know when or, for certain, where he died, but there is a strong tradition that it was at Monnington Straddel, now Monnington Court, just inside the Herefordshire boundary and within sight of Wales. This was his daughter's home. The poets do not seem to have accepted the fact of his death, for we have no elegy written to lament it, as we have for Llywelyn ap Gruffydd. But there was on this occasion little of the dumb despair that followed 1282. Glyndŵr had shown what could be done and another leader might well rise to do it. Many Welshmen refused to live under the anti-Welsh laws of Henry IV and became outlaws in the woods and hills, and known as *gwerin Owain*, Owain's folk. One of these lively spirits was Llywelyn ab y Moel, and his poems give us some idea of the life these rebels led. Graig Lwyd, possibly near the Elan valley, was their base, and in a *cywydd* 'To the Woods of Graig Lwyd' he says,

> . . .*Far better than wandering minstrelsy*
> *for one who's eager for goods,*
> *to take and unharness an Englishman*
> *under your branches, o fair region. . .*

Llywelyn ab y Moel was noted for his courage, but his account of how his band was routed by a troop of Englishmen, in his 'Battle of Waun Gaseg' is a lively and amusing piece of self-mockery. He wrote charming love poems to a woman called Euron.

Other poets wrote in protest against the new order. Dafydd ab Edmwnd angrily bewails the execution of Siôn Eos, a famous harpist, for accidentally killing a man in a brawl, in a *cywydd* which has the loveliest lines ever written about the harp. He was a man of landed family, a master of the craft of poetry and winner of the silver chair at the Carmarthen eisteddfod of 1451 for re-arranging and tightening up the twenty-four strict metres and for composing an example of each one. For those who loved soldiering there were the Wars of the Roses which, according to G.M. Trevelyan, were largely a Welsh affair. Guto'r Glyn was a Yorkist and wrote in praise of the Welsh Yorkist leaders. He praised Edward IV in verse and fought in France for the English king, but in the end it sickened him to see Welshman kill Welshman in what was basically an English quarrel. When William Herbert, Earl of Pembroke, invaded north Wales with fire and sword, Guto begged him to be merciful and not to wound Wales for the good of England. Guto, when not soldiering, was a wandering poet, well received in north and south Wales by noblemen and abbots whom he praised skilfully in *cywydd* and stricter measures. He turned his hand to cattle-droving too, and to lighter verse which is humorous and satirical. A man of his time, Guto'r Glyn steered a fascinating course through violence to a quiet, cared-for end, old and blind, in Valle Crucis Abbey.

Dafydd ap Gwilym's poems to women — real, achievable women — had become so popular that those who succeeded him, Bedo Aeddren, Dafydd ab Edmwnd and Dafydd Nanmor, may sometimes be suspected of inventing loves in order to compose in this agreeable convention. But twelve jurymen of Gwynedd (note the English legal system operating) had no doubts about Nanmor's intentions, for they banished him from north Wales for writing *cywyddau* to Gwen o'r Ddôl whilst her husband was away in France fighting for the king. He was well received in the south and wrote splendid poems in praise of patrons there. In the wars he favoured the Lancastrian side and wrote poems to Jasper and Henry Tudor. He loved to play tricks with his craft, versifying astronomy, astrology and weather lore. A famous *tour de force* of his is his *awdl* to Dafydd ap Tomas ap Dafydd, another of Edward IV's Welsh soldiers, in which he gives an example of each of the twenty-four old metres, proudly disregarding the modifications of Dafydd ab Edmwnd. Though Dafydd Nanmor claimed fidelity to Gwen o'r Ddôl, he is accredited with a lovely poem about the yellow hair of a girl called Llio, a poem which has characteristic images from art as well as nature.

As a young man Lewis Glyn Cothi was an outlaw in north Wales. He was learned, especially in heraldry, and his poems in praise of his hero, Jasper Tudor, more pleasantly called Siaspar Tudur in his own tongue, had prophetic elements, for the Tudur family offered much hope to Wales, even before this hope became finally linked with Edmwnd Tudur's son Henry, later Henry VII. And Lewis Glyn Cothi wrote the most heart-rending poem in Welsh, his *cywydd* on the death of his five-year-old son Siôn.

In the poetry of Siôn Cent religion takes the form of a severely moral, puritanical view of life and of those to whom life has been generous. He wrote a series of *cywyddau* to compare man to a day, on the dangers of the seven deadly sins, on the end of man's life in earth and the end of the world on Doomsday, on the illusion, the vanity, the worthlessness of this world and on the emptiness of man's boasting. Siôn Cent praises only God, Christ and the Trinity. For the noblemen of Wales he has only a fearful warning, couched in language stark enough to be immediately understood. As for the poets who praised the land-owners, for him they were just liars and flattering hypocrites.

The poets of the twelfth century had seen the beauty of the Welsh landscape, and much of the gnomic and prophetic verse had been set against a background of observed nature. A convention at least as old as the twelfth century had been that of the *llatai* or messenger. The poet, wishing to send a message, usually to a woman, pretends to ask a bird or beast to carry the message, and praises the creature chosen in lengthy description which displays his mastery of words and imagery. Cynddelw and Prydydd y Moch had sent fine stallions to greet a woman, and since stallions can carry human messengers this is perhaps not a conventional use. Dafydd ap Gwilym went further, into the realms of fantasy, in calling on the wind, the lark, the seagull, the cock pheasant, the eagle, the swan, the blackcap and the salmon to bear his messages. There had been no end to Dafydd's delight in the things of the countryside and for Llywelyn ab y Moel and Guto'r Glyn the woods had been a refuge. Now in the fifteenth century the observation of things animate and inanimate and the long-practised art of comparison-making were put to a social and practical purpose. A nobleman who wished to borrow something from a friend would ask a professional poet to put the request into a *cywydd* on his behalf, or the poet might write such a poem of asking for something he himself wanted, usually from a patron. Iolo Goch had asked for a stallion to replace his own, which had died. Llywelyn Gutun now asked in verse for a dog, for goats and for a pair of spectacles. Gutun Owain asks for a pair of hunting dogs on behalf of his patron's nephew, and gives a fine description of hounds in the chase. Tudur Aled writes to the abbot of Aberconwy to ask for a stallion for a friend and pens the most spirited description we have in Welsh of such an animal.

Some time near the middle of the fifteenth century, Ieuan ap Rhydderch wrote his *Gorhoffedd*, his exultation or poem of boasting, beginning his poem with a significant reference to Hywel ab Owain Gwynedd, perhaps the inventor of this kind of composition. I have suggested that such a poem could only have been sung in a time of comparative peace and in a settled society. Except for an occasional fearful eddy of the Wars of the Roses such conditions might well have obtained in west Wales in those days, so that it could have been possible for a cultured, well-to-do gentleman of central Ceredigion to tell us quietly how he became a polymath and a complete man. It was his father who had 'Llyfr Gwyn Rhydderch' written for him, perhaps by the monks of Strata Florida. Ieuan was familiar with the 'Mabinogion' and the poetry of both *Cynfeirdd* and *Gogynfeirdd*. He learnt what he called *yr eang Ffrangeg* (the spacious French); he could use the brass quadrant to tell 'the point of height of every star' and

> . . .the deep lowness of every depth
> to the distant world of Annwn,

thus linking medieval science with the old Welsh mythology. He has mastered the art of poetry and is good at all kinds of indoor and outdoor games and sports. There is no mention of war or military prowess in the poem. The nearest he comes to this is his claim to be good at archery, but only at a target.

As the year 1485 grew nearer, and during that year itself, the hopes aroused by the Tudur family brought more verse of political prophecy, but otherwise aggressiveness on the part of the poets is channelled into a kind of verse war, known in Welsh as *ymryson*, between two poets, an exchange of humorous or biting attacks which sometimes became a slanging match. Notable examples are those between Guto'r Glyn and Llywelyn ap Gutyn, Rhys Goch and Siôn Cent and, towards the end of the sixteenth century, Wiliam Cynwal and Edmwnd Prys.

The *awdl* and *cywydd* forms suitable for poems of some considerable length have already been referred to, but the shorter *englyn*, suitable for a kind of epigram and rather more unusually for a poem which is a sequence of *englynion*, has not yet been described. Different forms of *englyn* go back to the oldest Welsh poetry, but for centuries now the form known as *englyn unodl union* has most often been used. This is a poem of thirty syllables arranged in lines of ten, six, seven and seven syllables. Basically it has one end-rhyme, but in the first line one, two or three syllables overrun the rhyming word, and are echoed in the first words of the second line. Some form of *cynghanedd* is required in each line. Here is an *englyn* by an anonymous author of some centuries ago which I take as a statement of a Celtic *dolce vita*.

> *Englyn a thelyn a thân — ac afal*
> *ac yfwyr mewn diddan*
> *a gwin melys a chusan*
> *dyn fain lwys, dyna fyw'n lân.*

(*An englyn, a harp, a fire — and an apple/and drinkers in*

*merriness/and sweet wine and the kiss/of a slim pure girl, that's
the fine life.)*

Scene at an inn, perhaps? No, the sweet wine sounds
more like a patron's hall. Though the poet no more
had legal rights, there were landowners and prelates
who still welcomed a visit by a good poet and
entertained him generously. The records show Henry
VII paying a poet, whom the English civil servant
refers to as 'a Welsh rhymer', generously for a poem.
From Iorwerth Fynglwyd we learn a good deal about
the gentry of Glamorgan who were his patrons in the
first half of the sixteenth century. Poems of praise,
poems of asking (Iowerth Fynglwyd has a spirited
descriptive request for a ram, a randy animal, on
behalf of a friend), verse controversies, all these were
still fruitful matter for *awdl, cywydd* and *englyn*. The
tradition was brilliantly carried on by Tudur Aled,
Lewis Morgannwg, William Llŷn and Wiliam
Cynwal, and into the seventeenth century by Simwnt
Fychan, Siôn Phylip and Edmwnd Prys, though as
the sixteenth century advanced the poems became
more stereotyped and less inventive.

One profitable line of the sixteenth-century poet was
the provision of rhymed pedigrees for the upstart
Welsh gentlemen of the Tudor period, and Siôn Tudur
speaks scathingly of this practice. Once a member of
the Queen's guard in London, he was given the grade
of apprentice poet at Caerwys, but he felt free to put
aside the traditional mantle of the *prydydd* to entertain
his friends and patrons with satire, pastiche and
parody. His poems make good reading and the
Oxford Book Of Welsh Verse has four of them.

Some of the Tudor poets were well-to-do amateurs, as many of their predecessors had been. These were the Welsh gentry who, in the new Tudor age and in spite of Henry VIII's move to extirpate the Welsh language, continued to respect and nourish their country's cultural traditions. Other Welsh gentlemen went to London and prospered there, but in those mansions which were kept up in Wales the professional poets were no longer sure of a welcome, for all these changes had brought the grades of practising poets into disarray. The *clerwr* and the untrained versifier made the most of their opportunity, whilst the trained poets complained that they were not getting their proper due of patronage. Soon after coming to the throne Queen Elizabeth was informed by gentlemen of north Wales that this chaotic situation might lead to disturbances of the peace and she issued an order to three of them to organize an eisteddfod at Caerwys in 1568, at which poets and musicians should be examined and, if they qualified, be given permits to practise their professions. The order said,

Whereas it is come to the knowledge of the Lord President and other our council in the Marches of Wales that vagrant and idle persons, naming themselves Minstrels, Rythmers (sic) and Bards, are lately grown into such intolerable multitude within the Principality of North Wales, that not only gentlemen and others are oft disquieted in their habitations but also the expert minstrels and musicians. . .much discouraged in the practice of their knowledge, and also not a little hindered of livings and preferment. . .to require and command you. . .to cause open proclamation to be made that all and every person and persons that intend to maintain their living by name or colour of Minstrels, Rythmers and Bards appear before you. . .to admit such as by your wisdom and knowledges you shall find worthy to use, excercise and follow the Sciences and Faculties of their Professions. . .giving straight

monition and commendment in our name to the rest not worthy,
that they return to some honest labour. . .upon pain to be taken as
sturdy and idle vagabonds.

Before the end of the queen's reign another gentleman of north Wales, Thomas Prys, Plas Iolyn, son of
Dr Elis Prys, one of the three adjudicators at
Caerwys, was to use his freedom as a nobleman to
bring a breath of fresh sea air into the staling *cywydd*.
This adventurous landowner, one of the first three to
smoke tobacco publicly in London, was at different
times a soldier of the queen and a pirate. He knew
London well, not only its great houses but its tav-
erns, brothels and gaols, and he grew to hate the city.
He expresses this in an extraordinary *cywydd* to show
that London is hell, and he warns his son against all
officialdom. He was happiest in his remote hide-out
of Enlli, Bardsey Island, which he owned, or in the
merry company of poet friends at Llanrwst, not far
from his estate at Yspyty Ifan. One lively bilingual
poem bewails a misadventure at sea. In another he
sends a porpoise to carry a message to his cousin
and fellow-pirate Pirs Gruffudd, begging him to give
up piracy before it was too late. There was still life,
strength, invention, freshness and humour in the
cywydd, qualities which have carried it through as
perhaps the most frequently used and enjoyed of the
older verse forms in Welsh until our present day.

VIII

It is difficult and perhaps unnecessary to try to fix a time when the European Renaissance reached Wales. We have seen how, through translations mostly from Latin, the monks and the cultured gentlemen of Wales had kept in touch with European thought. Ambrose Bebb, in his brilliant study of the decline and dissolution of the religious houses of Wales, MACHLYD Y MYNACHLOGYDD, has suggested that early in the sixteenth century, under the learned Abbot Leyshon, Neath Abbey already knew something of the new wave of learning that was sweeping through western Europe. He finds evidence for this in the poetry of Lewis Morgannwg. What features of the Renaissance are we to look out for as we read Welsh prose and verse of the sixteenth and early seventeenth century, the age of the Tudors? Use of this phrase reminds us that it was the conquest of England by Henry Tudor which created effective links between Wales and the continent of Europe, for as Henry VII he commissioned the Italian scholar Polydore Vergil to write his *Anglica Historica*, which justified the Tudor monarchy internationally, and to produce an edition of the work of Gildas. Henry Tudor appointed an Italian, Carmeliano, as his Latin secretary — today we would call him foreign secretary — and he commissioned the early French printer, Vérard of Paris, to print him a *Lancelot* on vellum. All these contacts with the new learning, and other which were to follow, would be available to the Welsh gentlemen who surrounded Henry.

Medieval science and thought had become bogged down in late Latin, from which Renaissance writers broke away in two directions, one to the vernacular languages and the other to the earlier sources of European culture in ancient Greek. The use of the vernacular language, rather than Latin, by the poets of Sicily and Provence, and the development of French as a language for poetry, encouraged Cavalcanti and Dante to confirm contemporary Italian, and very simple Italian, as a literary language. In Wales there was no lack of respect for the Welsh language, which had an unbroken history of use in poetry, but the greatest respect had been for the most complex forms and the most erudite and difficult diction. The verse of the *clerwr*, the lowest order of poet, verse that was immediately comprehensible even to the illiterate, had not been thought worthy of recording in manuscript. As the sixteenth century advanced, writing in the so-called free metres, that is not in any of the classical twenty-four, became more acceptable and respectable, and a considerable body of verse of this kind, much of it included by Sir Thomas Parry-Williams in his CANU RHYDD CYNNAR, came to be written down and thereby preserved for us. It is to be noticed that some of the authors of this popular kind of verse, like Siôn Tudur, Wiliam Cynwal and Edmwnd Prys, also wrote in the strict metres and on the old established themes. Some of these free metres are clearly traceable back to old Welsh forms, others are borrowed from English lyrical forms. Edmwnd Prys, for example, gives us a lovely lyric in five long stanzas which he entitles 'Balet Gymraeg ar fesur About the Bank of Helicon' (*ar fesur* means *in the measure or metre of*). In this way, English airs and madrigals, used with elements of established Welsh versification, helped to inspire a new and charming body of lyrical writing. Wiliam Cynwal, in his defence of women against a spirited anonymous satire, chose a popular stanza form, since this kind of controversy was considered to be below the level of the strict metres. But Cynwal's stanza is of Welsh descent, as are those of the lyrics of Dic Huws and of the translation of the Psalms by Edmwnd Prys, stanza forms constructed from some of the simpler elements of the old prosody. Robin Clidro, a popular entertainer, used *cynghanedd* and simple stanza forms with cheerful freedom, much humour and keen social awareness. His 'Owdwl y Gath' (The Cat's Ode) begins with the very note of the travelling poet of the lower or *clerwr* order, prepared to entertain in tavern or hall.

> *Mae gen i awdl ffyrnig*
> *erbyn gwyliau Nadolig;*
> *rwy'n barod i'w chynnig*
> *o cha'i gennad i'w chanu.*

(*I've got a ferocious ode/for the holidays of Christmas;/I'm ready to offer it/if I get permission to sing it.*)

Cennad i ganu, permission to sing, is the term used by Mari Lwyd wassailers in Glamorgan up to this present century.

The art of poetry was becoming less esoteric. Gruffudd Robert, a Catholic exile writing in Italy, published in Milan in 1567, and in beautiful italic fount, the first part of his important analysis of the Welsh language. A true Renaissance man, he held that literature should be written in the contemporary language of the people for whom it is composed. He attacked the Welsh poets of his day for their conservative clinging to a frozen vocabulary. The contact with England had brought many English words into Welsh, but this did not worry Gruffudd Robert. If these words are in use, he said, and they are found to be useful, then use them in your writing, make them at home in your language. Sound advice, for this is something the English language has copiously and successfully done from French, and which Dafydd ap Gwilym did from English, French and Latin in the fourteenth century.

The effect of the rediscovery of Greek texts on Welsh literature is not so readily perceptible. For some years before the fall of Constantinople in 1453 Greek manuscripts, including versions of some of the great classics, were being brought to Italy, and 1453 produced a flood of texts and scholars. J.W.H. Atkins summed up the general effect thus: *In the first place, Greek studies had revealed human nature in the fullness of intellectual and moral freedom; and a heightened sense of the greatness of man and of the power of human reason therefore became general.* Such humanism was often in conflict with religion and some thinkers found difficulty in reconciling Platonism with Christianity, but the broadminded Pico della Mirandola looked on all pursuit of knowledge with equal respect. The conflict between humanism and puritanism, and their occasional fusing into one, are features of seventeenth-century Welsh writing.

The Trojan Hector had been known to medieval Welsh poets as a heroic figure, and Dafydd ap Gwilym had compared one of his loves to three famous Greek beauties, Policsena, Deidamia and that *famous, slim, fair Helen, who caused all the trouble between Greece and Troy.* Towards the end of the sixteenth century another gentleman poet, Thomas Prys, Plas Iolyn, who could afford to flout tradition, said that a girl he was praising was more beautiful than a whole bevy of Greek goddesses and legendary women, beginning with Venus, then new to Welsh poetry, and ending with Helen of Troy, taking in Cresyd too. Into his attack on women an anonymous satirist brought Medea, Berenice, Myrrha, Semiramis and of course Helen of Troy. Wiliam Cynwal, in his answer, ransacked the Bible and Christian hagiology for good women, before claiming Ceres, Isis and the nine Sybils.

One wonders how much the Welsh poets knew about Homer's ILIAD which, in the 1590s, was being splendidly translated into English by George Chapman. Probably about the turn of the century an unknown Welshman who, unlike even educated Englishmen of his day, could read and understand Chaucer and Henryson, put together in rhymed verse the powerful tragedy of TROELUS A CHRESYD, showing little or no awareness of Shakespeare's strange play on the same theme but introducing new elements in the trial of Cresyd by Priam and his sons and a scene where Calcas wonders whether he should escape from Troy and calls on Apollo for advice. TROELUS A CHRESYD, standing alone in the thin dramatic tradition of Wales, was unlikely to have been performed in public in its own day, and was certainly not printed until quite recently. A few Welsh miracle, mystery and morality plays have survived, but they are not associated with any particular cycle.

IX

The sixteenth century saw extraordinary developments in Welsh prose writing. Elis Gruffydd was born in Flintshire about the beginning of the century and set off to better himself in Tudor England. Eventually he spent most of his working life as an official in the garrison of Calais, where he copied Welsh poetry, translated a book on herbs from English, and an account of the labours of Hercules from French. And there he wrote his 'Chronicle', a history of Wales and England from the Norman Conquest to his own day, using his own experience of the wars in France at considerable length for the latter part of the book. He had no grand ideas about prose but wrote in a rugged, natural, idiomatic style, often bluntly amusing. The manuscript is important as history but, like TROELUS A CHRESYD, it could hardly have influenced anyone, for it has never been printed in its entirety, nor, so far as we know, ever copied until quite recently. For us now Elis Gruffydd stands like a weather-scarred monolith in a misty landscape, but he does give us a strong impression of how people spoke and wrote Welsh in those days, when they didn't have to please a patron. Passages from Elis Gruffydd will one day be required reading for students of history in Wales, especially as his book takes out of war and the politics of war whatever glamour these may have held, or still hold for some people.

The first printed books in Welsh were printed in

England, for there were no printing presses in sixteenth-century Wales. It is ironical that Queen Elizabeth, whose father had sought to 'extirpate' the Welsh language, should have resorted to that language to bolster up the new Protestant church. The Welsh people, or rather the Welsh gentry, for there was still no other public voice, were showing reluctance to accept Henry VIII's changes, or to give up what was known as the old faith. It is not likely that anyone has ever taken kindly to a religious or political faith compelled upon them from above. Officially it was thought, and here the queen's Welsh advisers must have been consulted, that if the Welsh were given the Bible and the Book of Common Prayer in their own language, they would be more inclined to accept the break with Rome. Though she showed no other sign of departing from her father's innovations and was prepared to countenance inhuman legal horrors to perpetuate them, she did unwittingly lay the foundation for a continuous tradition of splendid Welsh prose, and thereby secure the continued life of the Welsh language, which has since then proved to be not easily extirpable.

It is possible that even Henry VIII, at the end of his life, might have condoned a temporary resort to Welsh, for a year before he died a book edited by Sir John Prys, encouraged probably by Wiliam Salesbury, appeared. It is the first printed Welsh book and, since it bore no title, for the day of fanciful titles had not come, it is called by its first words 'Yn y lhyvyr hwnn' (*In this book*). The book is a mixed bag. It gives the Welsh alphabet, with comments on it, a calendar with hints for farmers for every month, Welsh translations of the Credo, the Lord's Prayer, the Ave Maria, the Ten Commandments and some verses from the New Testament, with a treatise on the Seven Deadly Sins. Sir John says (I translate),

Therefore it is proper to put into Welsh some of the holy scriptures, because many Welsh people can read Welsh without being able to read a word of English or Latin, and especially those matters which it is necessary for every Christian to know for the good of his soul.

This concern with the spiritual good and the morals of the Welsh people was to be that of educated Welsh gentlemen for a hundred years and more. Wiliam Salesbury, again in about the year 1546, produced a collection of Welsh proverbs, mostly put together by Gruffydd Hiraethog, which he called OLL SYNNWYR PEN KEMBERO (*All the Sense of a Welshman's head*)— the extraordinary spelling of *Cymro* is the fruit of Salesbury's classically influenced notions of orthography. In his preface he encouraged the Welsh to beg the king and his council for the Bible in Welsh. Salesbury also seems to have been the author of a petition to the bishops in 1552, asking to have the New Testament in Welsh and complaining of *the miserable darkness for the lack of the shynyng lyght of Christe's Gospell that styll remaineth among the inhabitantes of the principalitie.* Salesbury was worried about the quality of the Welsh spoken and written by the gentry of Wales of his own generation, and his purpose in publishing the old proverbs was to save for the future the wealth of words they employed. Saunders Lewis has called the preface to OLL SYNNWYR, *a manifesto of the Renaissance.* In 1547 Wiliam Salesbury published A DICTIONARY IN ENGLYSHE AND WELSHE MOCHE NECESSARY TO ALL SUCHE WELSHEMEN AS WIL SPEDLY LERNE THE

ENGLYSHE TONGUE, and dedicated it to Henry VIII. He followed this in 1550 with A BRIEFE AND A PLAYNE INTRODUCTION to the Welsh language for the use of merchants of the border counties who did business in Wales and young Welshmen brought up outside Wales. In 1551 appeared Salesbury's KYNNIVER LLITH A BAN, which had translations of large portions of the New Testament and which he intended for use in churches in Wales.

In 1563, in the fifth year of Elizabeth's reign, an act was passed requiring the five bishops to translate the Bible and the Book of Common Prayer into Welsh and to have copies placed in every church in Wales before St David's Day, 1566. It was to take much longer than this to translate the Bible, but in 1567 two very important books for churchmen appeared, Bishop Richard Davies's translation of the Book of Common Prayer, for which he consulted Salesbury, and Salesbury's own translation of the New Testament, done at the bishop's request and with his help in some of the epistles. I have already referred to Salesbury's strange orthographical system. Another practice of his was not to mutate initial consonants according to the rules, in order to make the meaning clearer to the unpractised reader. One of the difficulties of Welsh learners today is to find a mutated word in the dictionary. These peculiar ways of Salesbury's have aroused criticism from his day to ours, and they have tended to blind readers to the naturalness, the flow, balance and power of his prose. We owe very much to this descendant of an Anglo-Norman who came to Denbigh in the time of the ruthless Edward I. It is a pity that he abandoned the older Welsh forms of Ifan, Pawl and Moesen for Ioan, Paul (pronounced as in English) and Moses, and that he has been followed in this by subsequent translators.

William Salesbury and Richard Davies are said to have fallen out over the meaning of a word, and the translation of the whole Bible was undertaken by William Morgan and eventually printed in London in 1588. Founded on Salesbury's translation, but not accepting his idiosyncratic spellings, William Morgan's version does not so much aim to be comprehensive to the less educated as to martial the vast vocabulary of the Welsh poets into splendid prose which has lit the way for Welsh writing up to our own day.

In 1620 Bishop Richard Parry published a revised version of William Morgan's Bible, easing some of its stiffness into a more natural and idiomatic manner, with an occasional glance at the English Authorized Version of 1611. It was the cheaper 1630 edition, popularly known as Y BEIBL BACH, the Little Bible, which made this translation available to the ordinary people of Wales, brought great prose into poor homes and made it possible for Welsh people to discuss religion and politics in a language they had previously used only at home, in tavern or market. This was the foundation of the literacy of the Welsh; it continues to enrich their daily converation and it has preserved in common use much of the varied wealth of the language, a vocabulary which might otherwise have remained only in scholarly memories with the growing remoteness of poetry in the strict metres.

Morris Kyffin, comptroller of the queen's musters in Ireland, after publishing a poem in praise of the queen, 'The Blessednes of Brytayne', and a translation into English of Terence's *Andria* in 1594, published his DEFFYNNIAD FFYDD EGLWYS LOEGR, a translation from the Latin of Bishop Jewel's *Apologia Ecclesiae Anglicanae*. In his foreword to the Christian Reader Kyffin follows the advice of Gruffudd Robert in pursuing a direct and easily comprehensive prose style. He says,

Mi a dybias yn oref adel heibio'r hen eiriau cymreig yr rhai ydynt wedi tyfu allan o gydnabod a chydarfer y cyffredin, ag a ddewisais y geiriau howssaf, rhwyddaf, a sathredicca gallwn, i wneuthur ffordd yr ymadrodd yn rhydd ag yn ddirwystrus i'r sawl ni wyddant ond y gymraeg arferedig.

(I have thought it best to let go by those old Welsh words which have grown out of recognition and the usage of the common people, and I have chosen the simplest, easiest and most well-worn that I could, to make the way of speech free and untroublesome for those who only know current Welsh.)

The gentry and the clerics had played their part in bringing the tools of culture to the people of Wales, in making literature generally comprehensible.

X

The 'Beibl Bach' was meant for the common people of Wales, and so, in the seventeenth century, was poetry in the free metres, for it was being realized that the simple, singable stanzas, and the simpler language, offered a powerful medium for propaganda, religious, moral and political. Richard Hughes (Dic Huws in the manuscripts), for years equerry to Queen Elizabeth and then to James I, had written love lyrics and satires in these metres. And he brought into Welsh something of the spirit of the Elizabethan madrigalist. In a charming dialogue between the poet and the nightingale he has Cupid's dart in his breast, surely the first Welsh poet to have suffered this, and then he imitates the bird's song in these untranslatable words.

Pwy, pwy, pwy, och pwy a ddial
fy llwyr gam a'm gorthrwm ofal;
helped, helped, duw, duw, duw:
hi atebe, duw, yn ddiatal.

But this stanza form is the old *englyn cyrch digynghanedd*, which the fourteenth-century Einion Offeiriad had said was below the attention of a poet of the first rank, and which like the *triban* became a very popular metre. Edmwnd Prys, for his translations to the Psalms, used a four-line stanza which consisted of two *awdl gywydd* couplets put together, a form which as a result came to be known as *mesur salm* and for which our hymnbooks have scores of tunes. The lyrics of Dic Huws, and others of a similar nature by contemporaries of his, would seem to indicate a new direction for Welsh poetry, but sterner stuff was to come.

Rhys Prichard, vicar of Llanymddyfri, in pedestrian but powerful stanzas pounded the gentry of Wales for their over-indulgence in the pleasures of the flesh and the people of Wales in general for their immorality. This was the puritan face of the Church of England in those days. It is difficult to believe that all the luxuries, delights and vices the Old Vicar thunders against were available to many people in seventeenth-century Wales, but he gives sound advice to people of every age, on every aspect of life, to the godly and ungodly, to the father of a family, to the young man who goes courting, to the cattle-drover, to the drunkard and to the man about to pray. He seems to take a pious pleasure in detailing the threat of various wraths of God, particularly the plague. Vicar Prichard's collected verses, known as 'Canwyll y Cymru' (*The Candle of the Welsh*) were not printed in his lifetime, but in spite of this were well known throughout the country.

That was the reformist voice of the Anglican Church in Wales, but the Puritans who had broken away from that church had their popular poets too. Morgan Llwyd, more famous for his prose work, LLYFR Y TRI ADERYN, goes beyond reformist propaganda to a mystical statement of union with God which foreshadows the erotic hymns of Ann Griffiths. LLYFR Y TRI ADERYN (*The Book of the Three Birds*) was published in London in 1653, and is in the form of a conversation between the Eagle, the Raven and the Dove. The Eagle represents the republican government of its day, the Raven is the established

Anglican Church, whilst the Dove stands for Puritanism. In an answer to the Eagle's question about paradise the Dove answers that paradise is only for someone who can escape from his own will, his own cunning, his own ends and his own paths. Paradise is not far away: it is anywhere where God's love appears. But Morgan Llwyd's greatest prose is in an earlier work, LLYTHYR I'R CYMRY CARIADUS (*A Letter to the Loving Welsh*), in which he begs his fellow-countrymen to realize their situation and to awake in time; prose which moves from quiet persuasion to an ecstatic statement of the love of God. The balance and movement of some passages recall Iolo Goch and Siôn Cent rather than any earlier prose writer with the exception of Wiliam Salesbury and William Morgan. From his base at Wrexham, not from his home near Maentwrog, Morgan Llwyd preached throughout north Wales, to put into effect Cromwell's Act for the Better Propagation of the Gospel in Wales.

The banned Catholic Church, too, had already had its propagandist in popular stanza form in Richard Gwyn of Llanidloes, sometimes known as Richard White, who had attacked Protestanism in long poems he called *Carolau*. He wrote in the same measure as Edmwnd Prys's psalms, speaking with nostalgia of the old ceremonies and holy days, and with horror at their removal. Richard Gwyn was brutally martyred in the Beast Market at Wrexham in 1584 and was recently canonized by the Church of Rome.

A poet who seems to sum up most of the characteristics of his age is Edward Morris of Perthi Llwydion, Cerrigydrudion, a farmer and cattle-drover who mastered the twenty-four old metres and claimed to have been welcomed in the old manner at holiday times in some of the great houses of north Wales. He, too, showed concern for the moral welfare of his compatriots in easily understood verses of the popular kind. He wrote Christmas poems which he called carols but which sound to us rather moralistic to bear that title. One of them, written in 1688, is entitled (I translate) 'A Christmas Carol of Praise to God on the coming of King William'. But there is also a carol to Cupid, in which he tells us that he has written many poems to girls, and another in which he sends summer with a message to his love, a poem which has Aurora, Phoebus, the waggons of Apollo, Venus and a threat to cut off the head of Hydra. In a collection of his work a poem of advice to his maidservant comes next to one of thanks to a girl who sent him a valentine. A very remarkable cattle-drover.

Another versatile poet was Huw Morus, known as Eos Ceiriog, the Nightingale of the Ceiriog valley, where he lived. He, too, wrote in the old metres, but he also experimented delightfully in the use of *cynghanedd* in lyric stanza forms and wrote with freshness and ease of love as well as on social, religious and political themes. His linking of words into chains of assonance and alliteration is a fore-echoing of what Gerard Manley Hopkins was to do with English two hundred years later.

Ellis Wynne is chiefly remembered for his prose work GWELEDIGAETHEU Y BARDD CWSC (*The Visions of the Sleeping Poet*), published in London in 1703, a book in which he shows, as Saunders Lewis has indicated, the influence of L'Estrange's translation of Quevedo, of Milton's PARADISE LOST and of Bunyan's

PILGRIM'S PROGRESS. In it we pass from a street which Bunyan might have imagined, to Satan addressing the fallen angels. The compilation and style are original enough, but Ellis Wynne was so put out by contemporary accusations of plagiary that he burnt the concluding sections of the work. His prose is at once poetic, powerful and eminently readable. He describes the peace, decency and content of a street in the city of God, in contrast to the swearing, mockery, whoring and drunkenness in the city of the Enemy. A phrase from this description, *ffrio ffair, a'r ffrost, a'r ffrwst, a'r ffrwgwd*, demonstrates a word-linking which goes back through Huw Morus to the prentice work of medieval poetic aspirants. This is a trick which Ellis Wynne does not use too often in his prose, lest it should pall.

In the second part of Y BARDD CWSC occur a simple series of stanzas on death, again meant to be understood by everybody, verses which might lead one to believe that Ellis Wynne was the actual author of many of those popular stanzas known as *hen benillion* or *penillion telyn*, old verses or verses for the harp. These otherwise anonymous little poems contain some of the loveliest writing of the late sixteenth and seventeenth century, many of them perfect epigrams dealing with aspects of rural life and life in general. There are many hundreds of them and they are still being collected.

XI

The involvement of Wales in what is known as the Age of Reason in western Europe was not the result of a sudden importation of ideas from abroad. We have seen that the Humanist movement established itself in Wales in the first half of the sixteenth century. Out of humanism grew modern science, which, with its new view of man and of man's situation in the universe, was the foundation of the Age of Reason and its collateral Augustan Age in literature. The Elizabethan Humphrey Lhuyd, having devoted much time to medicine and archaeology, and having met Ortelius in Antwerp, produced a map of Wales and one of England and Wales. At the same time Dr John Dee, of a Radnorshire family, had been an astronomer and mathematician of international repute, a reputation somewhat tarnished by his inclination towards necromancy. David Rowland of Anglesey had translated 'Lazarillo de Tormes' from Spanish, but into English, not Welsh, thereby giving England its first picaresque tale and opening a rich vein of fictional writing that conditions were not ready for in Wales. In the seventeenth century James Howell applied his learning and his enquiring mind to national characteristics, to the nature and inter-relationship of languages, and to the historical events of his own day, all this in his English letters. When the Restoration came, Charles II made James Howell Historiographer Royal. Thus by their studies and their visits abroad Welshmen had become familiar with and had kept abreast of important cultural developments in Europe.

With the new toleration of religious differences after 1688, the quarrels, the persecutions, the escapes to America, all these disturbances to the life of the Anglicized rather than the Welsh-speaking Welsh, were things of the past; the Welsh people settled back into their traditional ways, whilst the stage was set for the Morris brothers of Anglesey and their friends to assess the worth of their country's traditions in a balanced, non-partisan way. From now on literature was to be no longer something produced for the intelligent gentry, in return for hospitality and patronage, but for the people of Wales, and a new literate public was being prepared for a new kind of writing. In the early 1730s Griffith Jones, a Carmarthenshire man who became rector of Llanddowror, opened a school in that village to train teachers, and by 1737 he had organized circulating schools, sending out teachers from his base at Llanddowror to every corner of Wales. His aim was to enable people to read the Bible and the catechism, and thereby to make them better churchmen, but the general result was to make the Welsh the most literate country people in Europe, and to lay the foundation of the basic Welsh rural and working-class culture, with its centres in chapel and smithy rather than in the great and now largely Anglicized houses of the land. Who then were to be the writers for this new age of reason, this widespread literacy? The most influential of them were without doubt the Morris brothers, Lewis, Richard and William, and their friends Edward Richard, Goronwy Owen and Evan Evans.

I have already suggested a Welsh background for the Age of Reason in Wales, but Saunders Lewis has carefully analysed the debt of these writers, in their critical attitudes, to what was happening in London and Dublin, and traced the urbanity of their humour and wit back to Dryden, Pope, Swift, the essayists Steele and Addison and the so-called Cockney translators of the classics. At the same time the Morris circle appreciated, and communicated their sense of the importance of the *penillion telyn* and of the poetry in the old Welsh metres, much of which was being rediscovered by them and in their day. Some of the excitement of these rediscoveries is expressed in a letter written in 1758 by Lewis Morris from his farm at Penbryn, near Aberystwyth, to Edward Richard. The Ieuan Fardd referred to is Evan Evans, of Lledrod, Ceredigion.

Who do you think I have at my elbow, as happy as ever Alexander thought himself after a conquest?   No less a man than Ieuan Fardd, who hath discovered some old MSS lately that no body of this age or the last ever as much as dreamed of. And this discovery is to him and me as great as that of America by Columbus. We have found an epic Poem in the British called Gododin, equal at least to the Iliad, Aeneid or Paradise Lost. Tudfwlch and Marchlew are heroes fiercer than Achilles and Satan.

The Morris circle exchanged letters in English as readily as in Welsh.

These letters are of great importance for the view they give us of life in eighteenth-century Wales and of the evolution of Welsh culture. Wales had no capital city, with clubs and coffee-houses where political and cultural matters could be discussed. Nor did Wales have magazines like the TATLER, SPECTATOR and GUARDIAN which could keep people in remote provincial isolation in line with new ideas in life and art. The letter therefore became the medium for such contacts and we are fortunate that so many letters of this period have survived.

Lewis Morris could turn a competent *cywydd* in the fifteenth century manner, but his most charming verse is in the freer stanza forms, which for him also had the aura of antiquity. Anthologies will give you such lovely poems as 'Caniad y Gog i Feirionnydd' (*The Cuckoo's Song to Meirionnydd*) with its praise of the girls of that county; 'Gallt y Gofal' (*Hillside of Care*) with its simple diction and *pennill* form; and 'Lladron Grigyll' (*The Thieves of Grigyll*), a spirited ballad on a contemporary theme. Yet his importance is greatest as a director and inspirer of others. When Edward Richard tried to get Evan Evans to translate Stanhope's CHRISTIAN DIRECTORY into Welsh, Lewis Morris wrote, *I wish Evans would leave such a common piece of drudgery as translating modern English books to some heavy brother of the Church that is fit for nothing else.*

Edward Richard, born at Ystradmeurig in Ceredigion, where he kept a famous grammar school, rigorously weeded out his poems so that very few of them are left to us. His best known poems are his pastorals, which he claimed were the first of their kind in the language. He wrote consciously in a tradition which went back through Spenser and Virgil to Theocritus, but his language, his stanza forms and the spirit of these poems are in line with experiments of the sixteenth- and seventeenth-century Welsh poets. An *englyn* of his on the death of an infant could be a Greek epigram in translation, but for the Welshness of its elegiac mood.

Goronwy Owen, who was born in a cottage on Anglesey and entered Jesus College, Oxford, as a servitor, combined, and all this is observable in his poetry, an interest in the classics, particularly the Roman Martial, medieval Welsh poetry and the poetry of the English Augustans. Livings in the Anglican Church took him away from Wales, to England and eventually to America, where he died in 1769, to be buried in his own cotton and tobacco plantation. He expressed his nostalgia for his birth-place in the strict metres and in language of con-trolled power. Writing of the Day of Judgement, he thinks of Anglesey.

> Pan fo Môn a'i thirionwch
> o wres fflam yn eirias fflwch,
> a'i thorrog wythi arian
> a'i phlwm a'i dur yn fflam dân.

(When Môn and its gentleness/from the flame's heat are one vast blaze,/its pregnant veins of silver,/its lead and steel one flame of fire.)

Evan Evans, known both as Ieuan Fardd and Ieuan Brydydd Hir, was taught by Edward Richard and encouraged to research into the old manuscripts by Lewis Morris. He was a formidable scholar in Greek and Latin, capable of such criticism as a comparison of the imagery of Cynddelw Brydydd Mawr and Homer. He translated old Welsh verse into Latin and English, and he showed both sets of versions to the poet Thomas Gray. A long correspondence with Bishop Thomas Percy, whose RELIQUES OF ANCIENT ENGLISH POETRY is one of the source books of the English Romantic Movement, shows how Welsh medieval poetry came to the knowledge of the literary antiquarians of that movement. Evan Evans's best known poem is a series of elegiac *englynion* lamenting the falling into ruins of the hall of Ifor Hael, friend and patron of Dafydd ap Gwilym, a desolation which he sums up in the line *mieri lle bu mawredd (thorns where there once was greatness)*. A poem expressing a similar nostalgia for past glories, and couched in equally astonishing *cynghanedd*, was to be written by David Davis, Castell Hywel, to the ruins of Ffynnon Bedr (Peterwell), outside Lampeter, where a fine avenue still stands and you may see, as I have done, bullocks graze in what remains of the parlour, as David Davis described them.

Before leaving this group of poets, which has been aptly designated a school of Welsh Augustans, I must refer to Richard and William, younger brothers of Lewis Morris. Richard Morris spent his working years as an accountant in London, but is chiefly remarkable for his manuscript collection of Welsh poetry, mostly in the free metres (edited by Sir Thomas Parry-Williams), and for having founded the Honourable Society of Cymmrodorion, which is still based in London and which today continues to encourage research into Welsh literature and culture and to publish the results.

The other brother, William, for most of his life a tax collector at Caergybi (Holyhead), was also interested in the copying of old manuscripts, but is chiefly noted for the wealth of information about life in Anglesey which is found in his letters. The Morris brothers, in these varied ways, did more than anyone to give continued life to the old traditions and they are really responsible for the fact that a young Welsh poet can and does today use any metre from *cywydd* and *englyn* to *vers libre* to react in a modern way to contemporary situations.

A great prose work was produced during the first half of the eighteenth century, DRYCH Y PRIF OESOEDD (*The Mirror of the Chief Ages*), by Theophilus Evans, who was born in the lower Teifi valley and spent his life as a cleric in Breconshire. First published in 1716, it was reprinted in 1740, with additions by the author and a much livelier rewriting of descriptive passages. The book is an attempted history of the Welsh, from the mythical beginning in the Tower of Babel, making Gomer, grandson of Noah, our ultimate ancestor (Gomer, according to the author, giving us the word Cymro) and on through the coming of the Romans to the penetration of Britain by the English. The second part gives an account of Christianity in Wales, from the first preaching up to the Protestant Reformation and the translation of the Bible into Welsh. By modern standards much of this is not serious history for, given a hint, the author will use his imagination to invent details of battle or conversation, but the descriptions are apt, the writing is clear, direct and almost colloquial, and, by imposing his own view on the material he achieves a pattern of historical development. A stirring passage is his account of Caesar's invasion of Britian, in which he tells how the Britons had set fearful, sharp-pointed iron stakes below the surface of the water, the dismay and confusion of the Roman soldiers as the steel points tore the bottoms of the barges, and the delight of the Britons watching on dry land.

Relieved of the political and religious excesses of the seventeenth century, which were beyond the interest of most Welsh-speaking country people, Wales, essentially a rural country still, was content with age-old customs and ways of life. With no centralized influences it was a land of small, almost self-dependent communities, each with a viable balance of agriculture, stock-rearing and the crafts, each with its local dialect and cultural flavour. Life was hard, but it had its pleasures, the many religious holidays, the fair-days pegged to seasonal change. (There are still people who will not sow potatoes before Tregaron's Ffair Caron.) Dancing and cock-fighting were popular, and a harpist, fiddler or ballad-singer always drew listeners in tavern or fair. This is the life which Richard Morris skimmed for lyrics and ballads in his delightful manuscript collection. But the ground was being prepared for change. Griffith Jones's schools brought a new seriousness to impinge upon the happy if thoughtless paganism of the country people, upon whom the Puritans and the reforming Anglicans had had little effect. Methodism was to alter the sound of things in Wales. The Morris circle looked with disfavour on the 'enthusiasm' of the new reformers, as though foreseeing the death of much that was happy in Welsh rural life and writing.

XII

From the end of the sixteenth century some members of the Anglican Church in Wales had been worried by the heedlessness of the Welsh people in the matter of the welfare of their souls. Now the number of such clerics increased. Llanddowror had taught people to read and they were the more prepared to listen to the message of Methodism, as the new movement came to be called, but it is important to remember that though breakaway chapels were built, the Methodist denomination was not formally constituted until 1811. If Howel Harris was the great leader and organizer of Welsh Methodism, though Daniel Rowland should not be forgotten, William Williams, Pantycelyn, was its great poet. Williams's hymns, now thought of as the first modern Welsh lyrics, were published by him as they were written, in a series of cheap little paperbacks, and became immensely popular throughout the country. Sir Thomas Parry-Williams divided the main themes of the hymns into three: the pilgrim, with both the PILGRIM'S PROGRESS and 'Exodus' in mind, on his way to the promised land of heaven, with much imagery of deserts and distant hills; then almost erotic references to God as the Darling (*Anwylyd*), sometimes as a lovely Rose of Sharon, sometimes a white lily and, finally, imagery of the suffering and death of Christ on the cross. All these themes are brought near to us by the simplicity and directness of the language, by our association of them with the hills of north Carmarthenshire and Williams's

missionary journeys on horseback, and by the extraordinary number of references to times of the day
and night in his poetry. Writing in 1863, Gwilym
Marles sharply remarked that there was never so
much talk about blood in any book written since the
beginning of the world. The new reformers stressed
the physical sufferings of Christ as man and god.
Howel Harris said that he and his colleagues
preached to the heat and the spirit rather than to the
reason. They carried conviction by stirring the soul to
its depths, whilst others, he said, left the soul quiet,
not searching into the heart. In this the Age of
Reason was ceding to the Romantic attitude, and
Williams's long poem 'Bywyd a Marwolaeth
Theomemphus' (*The Life and Death of Theomemphus*)
has been called the first great poem of the European
Romantic Movement. Published in 1764, it is the
story of a spiritual pilgrimage, with perhaps Howel
Harris as the pilgrim. In that case the Philomela of
the poem may well have been Madam Sidney
Griffith, whom Harris regarded as a kind of divine
mouthpiece of Methodism, whilst she thought of
herself as the prophetess or spiritual mother of the
movement in Wales. That there may also have been
a more earthly association between them is suggested
by the 'Farewell Song of Theomemphus', the culmi-
nating section of this fascinating poem. I translate
one stanza.

> *Be you married, be you widowed,*
> *be you married now in haste,*
> *and let seven men in succession*
> *own the fairness of your face,*
> *I will not be one amongst them,*
> *I have no desire to lie*

> *under the power of such pleasure*
> *whilst stars orbit in the sky.*

A more passionately erotic mysticism informs the hymn-lyrics of Ann Griffiths, of Dolwar Fechan, Llanfihangel-yng-Ngwynfa, a sudden convert to Methodism from the earlier, carefree delights of Welsh rural life. These poems were never published by the author, nor even left in manuscript by her. She recited them to her maid-servant who remembered them, so that they could be published, soon after the end of their author's brief life, by the maid's husband. Ann Griffiths's most famous hymn sees Christ standing among the myrtles, *a worthy object of my love*, and expresses the wish,

> *Hail! the morning*
> *I shall see him with no veil.*

The thought of the physical death of Christ gives her phrases of staggering irony, *putting the author of life to death*, whilst in another hymn she begs to become a green tree, planted on the shore of living waters.

It is strange that a conscious artist, as Ann Griffiths clearly was, should have felt so little urge to communicate her work. Some of her letters have survived, but only one of them, to her friend Elizabeth Evans, is in her own hand. The others are copies made by John Hughes, the preacher who became her spiritual mentor and confessor. These letters are an astonishing, though guarded, revelation of her agony of mind as she finds herself wavering in her new faith. She quotes frequently from the Bible and begs for speedy replies to her letters. She impresses us as a very lonely person who turns her back on this world in unfrightened awareness of approaching death, convinced that death will bring her the company of Christ. The letters have images of the same vivid suddenness as the poems. I translate.

It isn't strange that the sun hid its rays when its Creator was under nails. It astonishes me to think who was on the cross, he whose eyes are like a flame of fire piercing heaven and earth at the same time unable to see his creatures, the work of his hands.

Then a little later:

And thanks be for ever that the furnace and the fountain are so near each other.

I have mentioned the ballad-singers, important figures in the world Ann Griffiths turned her back on. Little printing presses had sprung up in eighteenth-century Wales, and the singer, having sung his ballad of old story, contemporary event or moral diatribe, was able to peddle cheap broadsheets of the songs to the common people who could now read them. Another form of popular literature so peddled was the *anterliwt*. (This is a word which derives from the Latin *interludium*, which had been used for a short, comic intervention between the two parts of a long medieval religious or moral play.) The miracle and mystery plays faded with the Reformation in Wales, but the *anterliwt*, as simply written as the old *pennill telyn*, continued to delight the ordinary people, especially those of north Wales, up to the end of the eighteenth century. It generally had a main plot and a sub-plot. The latter usually offered a battle of wits between the Fool and the Miser, and the Fool linked up with the main plot, which drew on an international fund of story, including the Bible. There was one on David and Uriah's wife, whilst another purported to present a chronicle of Welsh history from the Trojan Brutus to George III. There was much broad humour and the Fool entertained with songs and dances. As in the old moralities, the characters were types rather than persons. It must all have been great stuff for anyone who still couldn't read.

The names of some of the *anterliwt* writers are known, but the best and most famous of them was Thomas Edwards, known as Twm o'r Nant. The actors were amateurs who joined together to form companies for short seasons. Twm o'r Nant joined such a company as a boy of twelve, but in his autobiography he tells us that he had written poems and two interludes before he was nine years old. Twm o'r Nant raised this form of entertainment to a masterly, thoughtful and well observed presentation of man's condition, taking what is essentially a medieval moral and philosophical standpoint. His best known works are 'Tri Chryfion Byd' (*Three Strong Ones of the World*), 'Pleser a Gofid' (*Pleasure and Trouble*), 'Cyfoeth a Thlodi' (*Wealth and Poverty*) and 'Pedair Colofn Gwladwriaeth' (*The Four Columns of the State*).

There is artistry in Twm o'r Nant's versifying and in his use of *cynghanedd*. In his analysis of a passage in 'Pleser a Gofid', where Rondol, the Miser's wife, is dead and the Miser is persuaded by Pleser, the Fool in this play, to marry a shopkeeper, Saunders Lewis has shown the cunning blend of elements, satire, parody, irony and comic development which gives us something nearer to the comedy of Beaumarchais or Goldsmith than we usually find in the *anterliwt*.

Twm o'r Nant is a writer who has not yet been fully appreciated, perhaps because after him came a change of taste on the part of the public. There was more for people to read, the modern, competitive eisteddfod took the place of the acted play and, with the spread of Methodism, sermons took over the appeal of the acted morality, with its occasional bawdy laugh, and some of its acting too, whilst hymns replaced the old ballads and there were prayer meetings instead of country dance meetings. When I was a boy, 'Cân y Mochyn Du' (*The Song of the Black Pig*), an old Ceredigion pub song, was thought to be scandalously blasphemous.

Towards the end of the eighteenth century there appeared, this time in south Wales, a man whose influence on our culture was to be as great as that of Lewis Morris, to whose example he owed a debt. This was Edward Williams, who called himself Iolo Morganwg. He had no formal schooling and claimed to have learnt to read and write by helping his father, a mason, cut inscriptions on gravestones. But his mother was a cultured woman and the Glamorgan of his day had many poets and scholars. Iolo became friendly with some of them, and with the lexicographers John Walters and Thomas Richards, a fact which may explain his great interest in words. He worked as a stonemason in London and Kent, and in London he met members of the north Wales cultural group, the Gwyneddigion. His interest in old manuscripts and his evident scholarship led to his being asked to help Owen Jones (Owain Myfyr) and William Owen Pughe to put together THE MYVYRIAN ARCHAIOLOGY OF WALES, a great collection of our earlier literature which is only marred by the forgeries Iolo added to the manuscripts he collected and copied, and which were not detected until well into our present century. G. J. Williams, who revealed them in the course of a careful and sympathetic study of Iolo's life and work, believed that the stonemason had entered so fully into the literary traditions of Wales, and was so proud of them, that he could not resist setting his imagination free in such imitative writing, and some of the imitations which he fathered on Dafydd ap Gwilym are lovely poems in their own right, and it has been suggested that these poems would have been laughed at as anachronisms if they had been published under Iolo's name. Another reason for forgery was his urge to bolster up the claim of Glamorgan to equal Gwynedd in literary importance. When you go to the national eisteddfod today and see the procession of robed bards and the ceremony at the newly erected stone circle, you are witnessing one of Iolo Morganwg's inventions in action. He claimed an unbroken tradition of this kind in Glamorgan since druidic times.

Iolo's reaction to Methodism was to adopt the more rational humanist view of the Unitarians, and he showed much enthusiasm for the French Revolution. He urged the organized collection of words, idioms, folk sayings and folk poetry, and it is only today that many of his advanced ideas are being carried out by such an institution as the Folk Museum at St Fagans. An extraordinary man and a good poet.

Another Welshman who welcomed the French Revolution and who defended and advised the Americans in their breakaway from England, to be honoured by them for it, was Richard Price of Llangeinor in Glamorgan. His book, LOVE OF COUN-

TRY, makes a very clear distinction between national-ism and imperialism, but the book was written in English and does not come within the scope of this study. The first Welshman to write a revolutionary pamphlet in Welsh was Jac Glan-y-gors (John Jones), a farm servant of Cerrigydrudion, who became an innkeeper in London and a prominent member of the learned Welsh societies there. In his pamphlet 'Seren tan Gwmwl' (*A Star under a Cloud*) he addressed his fellow-countrymen in plain, straightforward Welsh, making a detailed and comprehensive attack on the British establishment, the Crown, the House of Lords, the House of Commons, bishops and priests. For him the American Revolution was the star of liberty, and he praised the French for following the American example. The two most evil things were war and taxation, and it was war that made taxation necess-ary. He concludes, and I translate:

It is evident that taxes are the greatest cause that the streets of London are so full of whores, and the parishes of Wales so full of poor people.

His final wish is a heavy conscience and unease for oppressors, success and happiness for those who wish their fellow-men well, unity and peace to mankind, justice and freedom to the world.

XIII

The work of Lewis Morris and Iolo Morganwg converged towards the end of the eighteenth century in the establishment of the eisteddfod as a central feature of Welsh cultural life, dominating the nature and form of writing in the old strict metres. It was with the encouragement and mentorship of the London-based society of north Walians, the Gwyneddigion, with the occasional attendance of Iolo Morganwg, that the eisteddfod became an annual event and a national institution, though it was not formally linked with Iolo's Gorsedd Beirdd, with its druidic paraphernalia, until the middle of the nineteenth century. The guiding spirits in the early years of the century, both in the writing of competitive verse and in their critical views, were David Thomas (Dafydd Ddu Eryri) and Walter Davies (Gwallter Mechain). Though London remained for decades the literary centre of Wales, much of this influence was spread by correspondence between interested persons and through the peripatetic siting of the annual eisteddfod, though the alternate swing from north to south Wales had not yet come into being.

The critical standards of Dafydd Ddu and Gwallter Mechain were based on the opinions and practice of Goronwy Owen, so that the neo-classical views of the Welsh Augustan Age were carried forward into the nineteenth and even the twentieth century. For Goronwy Owen the epic and the poem of praise were the highest modes and these required a diction exalted above common speech. For this purpose he recommended recourse to the old *awdl* measures, rather than to the more popular *cywydd*, and the early modern eisteddfodic insistence on this accounts for the greater prestige accorded today to the *awdl*, for which the chair is given, than to the crown given for the *pryddest*, which may be written in any of the freer forms, even free verse. Into the nineteenth century, therefore, there persisted the notion that rules could be laid down to govern content, form, style and diction, and that adjudicators at eisteddfodau should use these rules as their yard-stick. Goronwy Owen had admired Milton and William Owen Pughe now translated PARADISE LOST into Welsh as an example to the poets of what their aim should be. Pope and Johnson were equally respected, as poets and critics. Objectivity of view-point, good sense and correctness of language and metre, these the eisteddfodic poets were to be judged by, and competition was thought most suited to the production of poems with these qualities. Typical subjects for the *awdl* competition were 'Ystyriaeth ar Oes Dyn' (*A Consideration of the Life of Man*), 'Gwirionedd' (*Truth*), 'Brwydr Trafalgar' (*The Battle of Trafalgar*), 'Drylliad y Rothesay Castle' (*The Wreck of the Rothesay Castle*), 'Iwbili Sior III' (*George III's Jubilee*) and 'Amaethyddiaeth' (*Agriculture*). Virgil, after all, had written on this last subject. The best poem produced within these conventions was on the subject 'Dinystr Jerusalem' (*The Destruction of Jerusalem*) by Ebenezer Thomas, known as Eben Fardd, at the age of twenty-one in 1823. He com-peted later on such subjects as 'The Trials of Job', 'The Battle of Bosworth' and 'The Year', but never wrote so well again as for his first success. The subject for the Wrexham eisteddfod of 1820 was 'Hiraeth Cymro am ei Wlad' (*A Welshman's Longing for his Country*), which might be taken today to give an opportunity for the expression of personal feelings but, lest anyone in that day should think so, Gwallter Mechain said,

We imagine that the poets were not given this subject with the purpose of nourishing and increasing the undesirable emotion of nostalgia amongst our people when they wander away from their habitual home; but rather that their compositions might resemble so many treatises to advise the foolish, light-headed man from transferring himself and his family to a distant land.

In this sense Goronwy Owen himself must have been held up as an awful example. So, if the European romantic urge was strong in the work of Pantycelyn and Ann Griffiths, it was dogmatically banished from eisteddfodic verse.

But the eisteddfod declined in authority and in relevance to its age; romanticism had to come and criticism moved from the eisteddfod platform to the journals of the day, a situation with which we are now familiar. The pageantry of Gorsedd y Beirdd became a popular attraction, but music slowly ousted poetry as the main draw, so that today, apart from the show chairing, crowning and presentation of the prose medal, literature is degraded to a packed but rather insignificant tent.

Not all the poets confined themselves to competitive writing. The discipline in form and diction in such writing gave Ieuan Glan Geirionydd (another Evan Evans) a clarity and tightness in his poetry in the free metres. A deep personal feeling is expressed in a charming poem to the Llanrwst Free School which he attended as a boy. The epigram-hymn 'Mor Ddedwydd yw y Rhai trwy Ffydd' has a quiet, stoical perfection, whilst his magnificent 'Morfa Rhuddlan' brings an epic quality, with personal involvement, to a mood of melancholy and a haunting rhyme scheme which carry the mind forward to Verlaine's 'Chanson d'Automne'.

John Jones, who called himself Talhaiarn because he was born in the Harp tavern in Llanfair Talhaearn, became a church architect and spent much of his life in the pursuit of this craft in London and Paris. Though not successful in the eisteddfod, he wrote song lyrics which were much sung during the nineteenth century to some of the best known folk tunes. A lover of the good things of this life, and far from both Methodist reform and the academic interests of the learned societies, he translated Burns into Welsh and admired the work of Shakespeare and Byron.

He once wrote, and these are his own words, *I don't care a fig for philology and philosophy, I prefer llafar gwlad. Llafar gwlad* means country speech. Into a long poem called TAL AR BEN BODRAN, written in a stanza form borrowed from Byron's DON JUAN, Talhaiarn brings every side of his nature and writings, the humorous, disrespectful, cynical, gentle and the despairing. In one sequence of stanzas he goes deep into a cave in north Wales and finds himself in a hall of worthies, the great writers of the ages. A procession of pretty maidens, followed by a figure he recognizes as himself looking with interest at the girls, is led by his Muse, who approaches the three worthies Taliesin, Llywarch Hen and Aneirin and asks them whether Talhaiarn shall have a pedestal among them. But they all three turn him down. A mood of despair follows, and it was in such a mood that Talhaiarn killed himself in his birthplace, the Harp Inn at Llanfair Talhaearn.

Alun (John Blackwell, 1797-1840) had written poems of a lyrical nature, recapturing the immediacy and simplicity of the traditional *penillion*, and it was now, near the middle of the century, that the modern Welsh lyric came into existence. The inventor and first user of the Welsh word for lyric, *telyneg*, was D. Silvan Evans, in a collection called *Telynegion*, published in 1846. (The word derives from *telyn* (harp), as the word lyric does from the lyre.)   In these poems an even stronger link was forged between the earlier folk stanzas and the lyrical writing of the later nineteenth century. At the same time, Welsh writers, hardly at all affected by the first flush of English romanticism, show the influence of the lesser, more popular romantic poets, Thomas Moore, Mrs Hemans, Thomas Ingoldsby, before discovering Tennyson. There is an inevitable comparison to be made between Tennyson's 'The Brook' and 'Nant y Mynydd' *(The Mountain Brook)* by Ceiriog (J. Ceiriog Hughes, 1832-1887). R. Williams Parry pronounced this poem to be the most perfect lyric in Welsh, but for me, even though I recognize the masterly craftsmanship, there is something slightly comic in the notion of a portly station-master wishing he were like a little bird:

O na bawn fel deryn bach.

In his 'Alun Mabon', which Ceiriog called a lyrical pastoral, a sequence of poems which expresses his nostalgia for rural life, he gave the Welsh perhaps their most loved work, a blend of joy and gloom, in lyrics which are still sung and recited. What standards are we to apply? T. Gwynn Jones laid bare Ceiriog's slackness in grammar and versification. Saunders Lewis, whilst appreciating the metrical and verbal skill, has found in Ceiriog a lack of imagination and a failure to escape from the bourgeois values of respectable Welsh society. Ceiriog himself seems to have held little hope for the future of the Welsh language and culture, in spite of his words in the lovely last lyrics of 'Alun Mabon'.

A very different poet and near contemporary of Ceiriog was Islwyn (William Thomas). Heavily committed to eisteddfodic competition, Islwyn turned out thousands of lines in the strict metres on subjects that sound unattractive to us today, and with no great success. For us his most interesting poem sprang from a tragic experience of his young manhood, the death of a girl he was about to marry. In this poem, 'Y Storm' (*The Storm*), he uses blank verse, perhaps the influence of Wordsworth, to express a mystical view of man's relationship with the universe, based on the idea, not unlike that of Celtic paganism and Wordsworth's pantheism, of God's penetration of everything that is. *For everything is sacred.* Islwyn's faith in a future paradise finds happy and calm expression in such a hymn as 'Gwel uwchlaw cymylau amser' (*See above the clouds of time*). Though in revolt against the captivity of the old metres, his is the best thing ever said in their defence, when he aptly suggests how the search for a word to rhyme with another, or to fit into a pattern of *cynghanedd*, touches off another association in a kind of chain reaction of imagery. The line,

Chwilio am air a chael mwy

(To search for a word and find more)

occurs in a poem he wrote to Wales.

Islwyn's searching, meditative manner was new to Welsh poetry, and to communicate the subtleties of his thinking he created new compound words. And he seems to have been responsible for an artificial device which has since been used to distinguish between poetic and prosaic speech, the placing of the adjective before the noun, an inversion perhaps occasionally required by the more English rhythms of blank verse and the sonnet. An example is,

A dwyfol sobrwydd annherfynol fod.

XIV

The conditions which favoured the evolution of the English novel towards the middle of the eighteenth century were slow to be achieved in Wales, but in the 1840s a situation not unlike that of England, a hundred years before, came into being. In 1843 the newspaper-periodical YR AMSERAU was first published, to be linked in 1859 with Y FANER. Gwilym Hiraethog (William Rees) was its first editor and in it he published his LLYTHYRAU'R HEN FFARMWR (*The Letters of the Old Farmer*). In these he wrote in a natural spoken form of Welsh of the political, social and religious problems of his day, all from a radical standpoint, and all widely read. In 1877 came his HELYNTION BYWYD HEN DEILIWR (*The Troubles in the Life of an Old Tailor*). Here the narrator is the old tailor who, by virtue of his profession, visits all kinds of households and sits working in them long enough to sense the atmosphere of each house and to learn much about its occupants. The result gives us a view of the tailor's life, the story of a religious conversion, and a long account of the courtship of a farmer's daughter by a farmer's son and the upper class son of the *plas*. The farmer's son, being a chapel boy, of course wins.

Glasynys (Owen Wynne Jones), who worked in a quarry as a boy but became a clergyman, showed less interest in the new politics but wrote down in pleasant readable style his versions of ghost stories, fairy tales and other traditional matter of hearthside entertainment in north Wales. Some of these tales were published in a collection called CYMRU FU (*Wales that was*), which appeared in three parts, edited by Isaac Foulkes in the 1860s. This delightful collection, much of it written by Foulkes himself and later issued in one volume, became very popular reading in Wales and, bought by my father, was my own introduction to Welsh history, the old *penillion*, characters like Robin Ddu Ddewin, Iolo Morganwg, and the wealth and variety of Welsh tradition. This is still a lovely book to have and has not been rivalled as an anthology of prose and verse.

With this kind of activity in being, there was a public ready for the first Welsh novelist, Daniel Owen. Owen (1836–1895), son of a collier who lost his life in the Argoed colliery near Mold, received little early education but became a tailor, after being apprenticed to one of this craft. At the age of twenty-eight he became a Methodist preacher and went for a while to the theological college at Bala, where he read widely in English literature. After publishing sermons and sketches of Methodist personalities he was persuaded to write his first novel, Y DREFLAN (*The Little Town*), in 1879. This appeared chapter by chapter in a religious magazine called Y TRYSORFA, as did his next novel, HUNANGOFIANT RHYS LEWIS (*The Autobiography of Rhys Lewis*), in which he traded upon the popularity of biographies in his day. His subsequent novels, ENOC HUWS and GWEN TOMOS, first appeared, again chapter by chapter, in Y CYMRO, where he had also published the stories collected in 1895 as STRAEON Y PENTAN (*Hearthside Stories*).

In the opinion of Dr J. Gwilym Jones, a hard and fast Calvinistic religiosity, a belief in predestined salvation, a lack of broad sympathy for fellow human beings made Daniel Owen a satirist first of all, a condemner of men rather than a true novelist, since disapproval and contempt came more naturally to him than tolerance. He seems to have considered the poor to blame for their poverty and he had no sympathy for the trade union movement or for strikers. But he has his virtues; he is brilliantly in control of the style of his writing, modifying diction and manner to produce his desired, often ironical effects. He is a sharp observer and recorder of scenes of many kinds. His novels are still readable and characters he created, such as Wil Bryan, Thomas Bartley, Nansi'r Nant and Enoc Huws have become parts of our tradition. There is much truth in the lesson of Wil Bryan and the clock; you can take a thing to pieces but not always put it together again.

A periodical called Y TRAETHODYDD, founded by Lewis Edwards in 1845 and still appearing today, set out to raise the standard of Welsh taste and knowledge of foreign literatures, and to do this outside the circle of eisteddfodic influence. Lewis Edwards wrote thoughtfully and powerfully of the isolation of Welsh culture from the European heritage, especially in the case of the uneducated. No full appreciation of a writer, no standard of judgement was possible without awareness of what had happened and what was happening in other countries. He himself applied such a standard to the eisteddfodic poets of the nineteenth century and found them lacking. At the same time he was the first critic to see the greatness of Williams Pantycelyn, whilst showing little interest in poetry earlier than the eighteenth century. He believed in careful reading of poetry, with a sympathetic attempt to enter into the poet's attitude towards things. Poetry, he said, does not easily yield up its treasures, and, since literature was a means towards knowledge, the good poet should have something important to say. The audience for such poetry is necessarily small in any country, he believed; therefore popular poetry could not be high poetry.

One who took to heart Lewis Edwards's stressing of the need for Welsh writers to know something about the writing and thought of other countries was Robert Ambrose Jones, better known as Emrys ap Iwan. The fact that he had a French grandmother, though his father was a gardener at Bryn Aber, must have roused his interest in France and Europe. He abandoned gardening to study at Bala and became a teacher and preacher. In 1874, at the age of twenty-three, he went to a school of Lausanne to teach English and to learn French and German, and his readings in these languages convinced him of the importance of correctness in the use of a language. Myrddin Lloyd has shown that Emrys ap Iwan's priorities were purity of speech, then purity of words, then purity of sound. He poured scorn on those who brought English idioms into Welsh, but he had faith in the judgement of ordinary people in the choice of words. Religion and the native tongue were for him the foundation of a culture. Nonconformity, he said, had done good in spiritualizing religion, but much harm in separating the good from the beautiful. Taste had degenerated as a result. No literature could appeal to a whole nation if it was written from an openly sectarian point of view. Williams Pantycelyn, he said, though a Methodist, rose above or beyond this, and is therefore a great poet of the rank of Aneirin and Dafydd ap Gwilym, if not greater. Emrys ap Iwan's studies of the classics of Welsh prose have been instrumental in carrying on the tradition of good prose writing in Welsh. His own sermons are amongst the greatest in Welsh, and in these, and in his articles in the periodicals of the day, he castigated those faults he saw in the Wales about him.

The rediscovery of the old Welsh poetry in the eighteenth century and the new and more scientific interest in antiquities of all kinds were followed, towards the middle of the nineteenth century, by works of painstaking scholarship by men with little or no formal education. Thomas Stephens, a chemist of Merthyr, published in 1849 a very important work of criticism, THE LITERATURE OF THE KYMRY. Gweirydd ap Rhys (Robert John Pryse), who had only four days of schooling, became a famous weaver, taught himself English, Latin and Greek, contributed copiously to the GWYDDONIADUR, a Welsh encyclopedia, and in 1872 published his HANES Y BRYTANIAID A'R CYMRY, a very well documented and researched history of the Britons and the Welsh. The book was handsomely produced, with a wealth of engravings, by William Mackenzie of London, who paid the author the considerable sum of £360 for the book.

XV

During the last decades of the nineteenth century a group of poets came to be known as *Y Beirdd Newydd*, the new poets, since they wrote a more contemplative kind of poetry than the eisteddfod had been producing. They withdrew from reaction to natural stimuli, saw impermanence in the physical world, but did not achieve much newness until Elfed and Eifion Wyn appeared. Elfed (Howell Elvet Lewis) brought a lightness and delicacy to his discovery of Welsh mythology in GWYN AP NUDD and LLYN Y MORYNION, which he published in 1895. In 1906 Eifion Wyn (Eliseus Williams) published his TELYNEGION MAES A MÔR (*Lyrics of Field and Sea*) in which he returns to a simple delight in nature and a personal involvement in the seasons. In a later volume, a poem on the gypsy, 'Y Sipsiwn', shows a sensitive, perhaps sentimental, interest in a wanderer who is closer to nature than the poet finds himself. It is to be noted that Eifion Wyn never allowed his delight in nature to enter into conflict with his religion. Open paganism came from other, considerably greater, poets who were to dominate the first half of our present century.

There had been clearly romantic elements in the ideas of Lewis Edwards and in the work of the so-called New Poets, but the true romanticism of the turn of this century, comparable in many ways with what occurred in France and England a hundred years before, was launched by John Morris Jones, who later acquired a hyphen and a knighthood. We are indebted to Professor Alun Llywelyn-Williams for his analysis of this new romantic poetry in his book Y NOS, Y NIWL A'R YNYS. At Oxford John Morris Jones had come under the influence of Sir John Rhŷs's studies in Celtic mythology. Up until this time, Wales had known more antiquarians than historians. At the turn of the century, dissatisfaction with the contemporary state of things, especially in education, found justification in the Wales of the past, and a new patriotism of a romantic rather than rationalized nature came into being. There was satire of middle-class materialist values, as well as of the bogus antiquarianism of Gorsedd y Beirdd, which now controlled the National Eisteddfod. The medieval romances were studied and Celtic mythology offered a new range of subject matter.

The attitude to nature changed, bringing these new poets closer into line with Dafydd ap Gwilym's involvement in seasonal change. John Morris-Jones said: *The sensation is the subject, and nature is only the means of its expression, or the occasion for it.* Turning away from industry and the towns they found a primitive innocence in rural life, an innocence which we know is rarely there. Rousseau's notion of the noble savage was now reflected in a cult of the common man, elements of which are to be found in the verse of Eifion Wyn, Elfed and W.J. Gruffydd. A distaste for the greyness of late Victorian Wales made attractive the thought of a distant paradise, not the Christian one but a magical island which is a feature of Celtic tradition and which we get in W.J. Gruffydd's YNYS YR HUD, T. Gwynn Jones's 'Ymadawiad Arthur' and other poems. A new kind of love poetry was now being written which brought love into direct opposition to religion, as a protest against the limiting puritanism of the years back to the Methodist Revival. In 1900 W.J. Gruffydd and Silyn (Robert Roberts) published a volume called TELYNEGION, a collection of lyrics of love and nature. Silyn had won the prize at the Blaenau Ffestiniog eisteddfod of 1898 for 'Six Love Lyrics', a surprising subject which showed the growing influence of John Morris Jones. It is difficult for us today to realize how shocking lines like the following must have sounded then.

> Anwylach na'm henaid anfarwol
> I mi ydyw Olwen, fy mun.

(Dearer than my immortal soul/to me is Olwen, my girl.)

A similar confrontation of love and religion is expressed in W.J. Gruffydd's 'Trystan ac Esyllt' (an eisteddfod subject at Bangor, 1902).

> Mwy nag uffern, mwy na nef
> Ydoedd Esyllt iddo ef.

(More than hell, more than heaven/Esyllt was to him.)

Gruffydd regrets the vanishing of the old gods just as Swinburne bewails the triumph of the 'pale Galilean', whilst Silyn edges back towards reason and morality, as befits a Methodist preacher and a socialist reformer. But if religion carries with it the promise of a life to come, at least for the chosen, love goes with the certainty of despair and death.

Gruffydd's 'Trystan' bristles with examples of the tiresome trick of inversion to which I have already referred, phrases like *gwylltion lygaid* and *fy mlin serch*, which became a kind of poetic diction in the work of these poets, with Elphin, an interesting poet, as the worst offender. This happened in spite of the careful study and purification of the language by Sir John Morris-Jones, about whose work in this direction I can do no better than quote from Dr Thomas Parry in a note in his OXFORD BOOK OF WELSH VERSE: *Morris-Jones's works introduced into Welsh poetry a new purity of diction and clarity of style. . .and the high standard of twentieth century poetry is due very largely to his example and precept.*

In the second half of the nineteenth century Welsh scholars had been much influenced by German ideas and work in the fields of divinity, philosophy (Hegelism chiefly) and Celtic studies. Another influence was the accepting of the views of Ruskin and William Morris on the function of poetry by Morris-Jones at Oxford. Heine and Omar Khayyám had been translated into English and John Morris-Jones now undertook the translation of the Persian poem and some of the lyrics of Heine into Welsh. The paganism of THE RUBÁIYÁT suited the anti-puritanism of the newest poets and Morris-Jones's choice of Heine's lyrics to translate is interesting, for he went especially for lyrics of the pains of love. However, an original poem of his, 'Gwylanod' (*Seagulls*), departs beautifully from this gloomy view.

A greater poet within this movement was Thomas Gwynn Jones, the most skilful handler of *cynghanedd* for many centuries and a daring experimenter in metrical form. His 'Ymadawiad Arthur' (*The Departure of Arthur*) has already been mentioned as leading the way for the poets to the Celtic past and escape from the discouraging present. It should be remembered, however, that the subject might not have been set at the eisteddfod of 1902 but for Tennyson's widely popular attempt to present the Celtic hero as a Victorian gentleman, and that Gwynn Jones's approach to the story was through Tennyson and Malory rather than any Welsh source. His exploration of Celtic story took him to Afallon and Broseliawnd, over the fearful Atlantic with Madog, to Brittany again in 'Anatiomaros' and to the mythical Tir na n-Óg beyond Ireland, everywhere displaying his nostalgia for the Celtic past. He sums up this past in a long poem called 'Gwlad Hud' (*Land of Enchantment*) in which his longing is also for the gods of the past. I translate the last four lines.

> *Yet there, there, once*
> *I saw life of the fairest muse,*
> *I drank the nectar of the earth gods,*
> *gods of the dream of the morning.*

At the ruins of Bro Gynin, Dafydd ap Gwilym's birthplace, he sees life as an hour between two long forgettings, and for him the grave is a place of peace and forgetfulness, though he sees the possibility in 'Y Bedd' (*The Grave*) of a dream coming there that language cannot convey.

Dr Derec Llwyd Morgan has drawn our attention to the bitterness that underlies Gwynn Jones's nostalgic poetry. In despair, the poet withdrew from serious contemplation of the world about him. His disgust with what was being written in his own day is crystallized in an epigram 'Bawenyddiaeth', a title in which he makes the word *awenyddiaeth*, meaning the practice of the muse, begin with the word 'baw' (*dirt*). His own writing is so full of art, of the mastery of his craft, that we may too often be lulled into uncritical acceptance or insufficient understanding of what he has to say. But he did not turn his back entirely on the present. He hated the notion of capitalism and expressed this in his sonnet on a coal-mine disaster, 'Senghenydd'. And one of the happiest and lovelist poems of this century is 'Cân y Medd' (*Song of the Mead*), which has been aptly set to music and sung by Dafydd Iwan.

W.J. Gruffydd, realist, romantic and sharp satirist, continued to write verse in these different modes, his voice growing sharper as he aged, but to some his most memorable piece of writing is a prose passage in the second paragraph of his memoirs, HEN ATGOFION, published in 1936. Here he describes how, after driving through a rainy night from Cardiff, he was suddenly confronted with a view of Snowdon in starlight. He stopped to look at the majestic scene and in a sudden flash of vision realized how foolish he had been to have been hurt by the prejudice of critics, prejudice directed at others as well as himself.

A younger member of this group of followers of Sir John Morris-Jones was Robert Williams Parry, who broke away in more ways than one from the example of his elders. His Ten Commandments to young Welsh poets are terse, self-critical, salutory and amusing. The first commandment is to write strong prose of a Welsh nature: if you fail in this, turn to the easier old metres of versification. The last is, avoid the company of poets; ordinary mortals are much more interesting. He recommends life rather than literature as a source of inspiration, discourages competition but gives advice if you must; encourages the reading of foreign literatures, especially English; advises against the use of literary or archaic language, including words he had already used himself, whilst eschewing artificial simplicity.

Williams Parry almost totally disregarded the new fields of Celtic mythology opened up by Sir John Rhŷs and Sir John Morris-Jones, preferring to depend on his own experience of friendship, love, and wild and human nature. Of his few references to the Celtic past, 'Cantre'r Gwaelod' is no more than a lovely poetic excercise, whilst a later poem, 'Dyffryn Nantlle Ddoe a Heddiw', dismisses rather than recalls a legend. He is much more apt to find an echo to his thought in Greek mythology, as did Keats, whom Williams Parry much admired. In 1911 he made the pronouncement that: *The calls of flesh and nature have not had enough fair play at the hands of Welsh poets*, and he protested against *gormes y loywach nen*, the oppression of the brighter heaven, the tendency of puritanical Wales to offer consolation for the trials of this life in the promise of a paradisal life to come. His is a pagan attitude, for I take a pagan to be one who enjoys his heaven and faces his hell in this world of ours. In two sonnets called 'Gadael Tir' (*Leaving Land*), Williams Parry faces death with a request to Christ, who himself loved *the acres of solitude after dark*, to grant the poet

> Ryw uffern lonydd, leddf ar ryw bell ros,
> Lle chwyth atgofus, dangnefeddus wynt
> Hen gerddi gwesty'r ddaear garodd gynt.

(*Some quiet, plaintive hell on some far moor, | where a remembering, peaceful wind will blow | old songs of the earth's inn which he once loved.*)

In 1910 he won the National Eisteddfod chair for his long and beautifully written *awdl* 'Yr Haf' (*Summer*) on the delights and torments of love against a background of the revival of nature in spring, but it was not long before he parodied his own poem in 'Yr Hwyaden' (*The Duck*), where the lovers are a wild duck and her drake and where he pillories his own tricks of style and the inflated language he was abandoning.

Only Dafydd ap Gwilym has written as well about the fox as Williams Parry has done, and no one as well as he about the cock pheasant, the curlew, the wood-pigeon, the weasel, geese and heifers, and that with a countryman's knowledge and without senti-mentality. There is wit and deep feeling in his lyrics and sonnets to friends, and he shows concern and anger at the academic betrayal of Saunders Lewis after the fire at Penyberth airfield. This event, and the coming of World War II, affected him rather as the Easter Rebellion did Yeats, and Williams Parry's later verse is bitter and disillusioned. In a poem written in 1937 he calls on the sun to stand still and let the crowbars of the grass destroy man and his works.

The 1914–18 war dealt a blow to the partially roman-tic writing we have been considering, though Alun Llywelyn-Williams sees in the work of Crwys and J. J. Williams a continuing romanticism of the chapel, more in line with the simple, beautifully phrased and easily understood lyrics of Eifion Wyn. Cynan (Sir Albert Evans Jones) had a flavour of this, too, but his long poem in 8-syllable couplets, 'Mab y Bwthyn' (*Son of the Cottage*), which has been seen as an account of the loss of innocence, brought something new in the form of direct reportage from the trenches and *estaminets* of Flanders, exciting stuff when it appeared in 1920. Hedd Wyn had written his unforgettable lyric on the pity and horror of war before dying in France and thus failing to keep his appointment with the chair he had won at Birkenhead in 1917.

But already a new, anti-romantic voice had spoken in astringent avoidance of poetic diction, that of T. H. Parry-Williams (later Sir Thomas), yet another poet from Snowdonia, born this time within sight of the summit, at his grim, much loved Rhyd-ddu. For the Bangor eisteddfod of 1915 the subject for the crown had been left open and Parry-Williams chose for himself 'Y Ddinas' (*The City*), in a blank verse poem which arose from his year in Paris as a postgraduate student at the Sorbonne. No serious treatment of city life had been attempted in Welsh since Thomas Prys's *cywydd* to London; now in 'Y Ddinas' we are given despairing but sympathetic accounts of a worker, an artist and a prostitute in a city which induces corruption and suicide. It does not surprise us that Eifion Wyn, one of the three adjudicators, strongly condemned the poem but yielded to the approval of the other two.

A thirty-minute radio poem by Parry-Williams, 'Esgyrn y Gynnen' (*The Bones of the Contention*) analyses the pros and cons for a pride in Wales and the Welsh language. A similarly aloof analysis on a smaller scale in 'Hon' breaks down in a passionate statement of instinctive love of country, which for him was an extension of his love for Rhyd-ddu and its surroundings. In sonnets, epigrams and other short poems his restless, dissecting intelligence probes his own experiences and the condition of man in this world. Like his cousin Williams Parry he abandoned the dream of a happier life to come, and in a poem 'I'm Hynafiaid' (*To My Forefathers*), in which he shows content with the little he has inherited, he says,

> *Mi gefais gennych greigiau dan fy nhraed,*
> *A'u holl doethineb bagan yn fy ngwaed.*

(From you I received rocks under my feet, / and all their pagan wisdom in my blood.)

Throughout his work Parry-Williams shows a dry wit and stubborn humanity, expressed with consistent certainty in rhythm and language. His effect on the writing of Welsh has been like that of T. S. Eliot on English. In his essays, where one gets the most readable and craftsmanlike prose of this century, we find a similar attitude to himself and to life, and a similar certainty and variety of expression.

XVI

When the writers of the turn of the century in Wales wrote in admiration of the ordinary country people they did so from intimate knowledge, for they were all of humble origin, unlike Ruskin and William Morris in England, but it was Owen M. Edwards who first wrote and published specifically for literate country people and industrial workers. A brilliant historian, and fellow of Lincoln College, Oxford, he directed his famous periodical CYMRU towards anyone who could read and was interested in his or her country. At the same time he was very ready to accept articles from such readers. He produced magazines for children too, and, for those people eager to learn more about Welsh literature but without access to university libraries, a series called CYFRES Y FIL (*The Series of the Thousand*), attractive little books, each concentrating on one writer, which were within the reach of any pocket. It was from one of these, bought by my father, that I caught my first sense of the grandeur of Iolo Goch. Whilst fully aware of the glories of past Welsh writing, O. M. Edwards himself wrote clear, contemporary but little polluted prose, to give his many readers accounts of his travels in Wales and Brittany, and of his own education, with good stories of Oxford, in CLYCH ADGOF (*Bells of Memory*), again in the CYFRES Y FIL series. We owe much to the unacademic behaviour of this academic.

Lacking the leisured middle class which fostered the growth of the novel in England and in parts of Europe, the novel languished in Wales after Daniel Owen. In the early decades of this century, and even more recently, fiction has been considered worthless because it is not true. But the short stories and novels of Dr Kate Roberts, (1891–1985), are certainly true of the grim poverty of the north-west of Wales which she remembers from her childhood. Although strongly nationlist, she never allowed her political opinions to condition her view of mankind. I have spoken of the effect of certain events in 1936 on R. Williams Parry. After 1936 there came a long gap in Kate Roberts's writing of fiction, a time perhaps when she was adjusting herself to those events and to the coming of war. Before this hiatus in her creative work she had written of the sufferings and of the tragic misunderstandings in the lives of others. Now her fiction becomes more psychological; it deals with people more like herself and her own sufferings are involved. In 1958 she wrote, and I venture to translate,

In my later years I have had to go through bitter experiences alone, and the only way to be able to live at all was to write, not about those things as they happened to me but to write about other kinds of suffering and to give them to other kinds of people. Suffering itself can turn to a kind of joy. . .to talk about people who go to the depth of suffering, who drink the bitter dregs and rise again, not victorious but with confidence to face life once more.

Though Kate Roberts's view of life is grim and painful, she remains conscious of liveliness and dignity in the human race. Her gradual, deliberate mastery of the craft of fiction has made her the outstanding Welsh novelist of this century.

A more cheerful view of life, though again as rural in background as Kate Roberts's early work and as backward looking, is that of D. J. Williams, in his short stories, his memories of his native north Carmarthenshire and his autobiographical writing. HEN DŶ FFARM (*An Old Farmhouse*), the first part of his autobiography, has been translated into English. His prose style is rooted in the racy Welsh of his region and he keeps a severe check on himself in the employment of literary devices. He writes of the past and its fullness, and his delight in these memories is tinged with bitterness at the thought of what we have lost in Wales, with very little to take its place. D.J. (there is only one D.J.) was one of the three fire-raisers of Penyberth, a warm-hearted, companionable man it did one good to meet.

Another notable writer of fiction and a prolific writer of books for children was E. Tegla Davies. TIR Y DYNEDDON, which appeared in 1922, is a fantasy highly praised by the critics, but which Saunders Lewis has found to be tainted with the same 'mil-dew of evangelicism' as he has found in Tegla's other works. (This writer is generally and affection-ately referred to as Tegla.) Better known, and already thought of as a classic, though the same 'mildew' is there, is a novel called GŴR PEN Y BRYN, which has been translated into English as THE MASTER OF PEN Y BRYN. Of chapter XI in this novel Sir Ifor Williams said that the story of the sheep-killing dogs was beyond compare in our literature.

Another interesting novelist, and a good poet too, was T. Rowland Hughes. His best known novel, O LAW I LAW, ingeniously traces the interactions of a community through a series of pieces of furniture which are sold privately, not on auction, a method of sale which is indicated by the title. In another novel, WILLIAM JONES, and this was something new for Welsh fiction, he takes us into the cultural set-up of the industrial valleys of south-east Wales, where his anti-hero, a very ordinary, nice north Walian, discovers that the people of the south can be quite decent human beings after all. For me this novel is marred by outmoded conventions, if we take the novel as an international form, the obtrusive 'dear reader' attitude of the author, and his pretence that he is not responsible for the behaviour and ideas of his characters, since that was how things happened.

The literature and politics of the middle fifty years or so of this century have been dominated by the frail figure and keen intelligence of Saunders Lewis. His political writings have been in favour of Welsh nationalism, and he was president of the party now known as 'Plaid Cymru' from 1926 to 1939. It was his radio talk, 'Tynged yr Iaith' (*The Fate of the Language*), which drew urgent attention, especially on the part of young people, to the desperate plight of the language and which inspired the movements which have already resulted in a far wider use of Welsh.

Saunders Lewis's two short novels are both studies of young women, MONICA (1930) and MERCH GWERN HYWEL (1964). Monica, uprooted to a Swansea suburb and with no sense of community, finds that the sexual act alone does not make a happy marriage, a recurring theme in this author's work. This study of a woman isolated by her up-bringing from tradition and its decencies and declining to despair and death, her husband having caught a veneral disease from a prostitute, was new and shocking for many respectable readers when it appeared, but Islwyn Ffowc Elis has shown its similarity to the DUCTOR NUPTIARUM of Williams Pantycelyn. The love affair and marriage of Sarah Jones of Gwern Hywel is, on the other hand, set in an integrated society and against the background of the establishing of the Methodist Church in Wales.

Drama has proved Saunders Lewis's most successful medium, with a dozen plays to his credit, dealing with the necessary power of tradition, a proud sense of responsibility towards one's forebears, the conflict between deep personal urges and authority, the need for self-sacrifice and the insufficiency of the sexual impulse. Blodeuwedd, heroine of the play of that name, has been made of flowers by the magician Gwydion, has no sense of human or social loyalty and unthinkingly but passionately betrays her husband and plots his killing. In SIWAN again the wife is unfaithful, but comes to realize the necessity to subdue her instincts to the social, dynastic need. Similar tensions and conflicts are worked out in what has become the most important body of drama in Welsh. Saunders Lewis's poetry is comparatively small in quantity but of the highest importance. The Catholic faith to which he was a convert gave him the mood and matter of such lovely poems as 'Difiau Dyrchafael' (*Ascension Thursday*), 'Mair Fadlen' (*Mary Magdalen*) and the agony of 'Gweddi'r Terfyn' (*The Ultimate Prayer*). His ode on the death of Sir John Edward Lloyd is one of the great European poems of this century.

In the field of criticism Saunders Lewis has touched upon nothing, old or new, without throwing new, often staggeringly new light on it.

There has never been so much activity, on such a broad front of writing, in Wales, as we have seen during the past few decades. All I can do, therefore, from now until the end of this book is to continue with the principle of selecting writers of outstanding significance, whilst avoiding the temptation of listing other good writers, only to dismiss them with an inadequate epithet.

D. Gwenallt Jones (1899–1968), usually known as Gwenallt, has been of all the poets of this century in Wales the most aware of the contemporary situation and the most prepared to face it in his poetry, something which his great predecessor, T. Gwynn Jones, did uncharacteristically in 'Senghenydd'. (Gwenallt's keening lament, 'Trychineb Aberfan' (*The Aberfan Disaster*), refers back to the frightful loss of life at Senghenydd.) Gwenallt moved, with passion and often with fury, through socialism, pacificism and nationalism to a complete acceptance of Christianity and a profound sense of his own sin. He sees the Wales which persisted until it was corrupted by capitalism and industry as the product of Christianity and his nationalism is often couched in terms of a return to the faith. He himself experienced the effects of industry on the landscape and people of the Swansea valley, and he expresses his detestation of what has happened in south Wales.

In his work we see sense images transmuted into symbols in a direct, uncomplicated way, and his own sin is stated in remarkable poems on animals, 'Y

Twrch Trwyth' (the Wild Boar of Celtic legend), 'Y Draenog' (*The Hedgehog*), 'Y Sarff' (*The Serpent*) and 'Y Ffwlbart' (*The Polecat*). A powerful poem on Christianity, 'Y Gristionogaeth', exemplifies his skilful use of *cynghanedd* in the freer metres. His craftsmanship, often daring and effective in its blending of elements, is not always consistent, but it is the intensity and honesty of his reaction to the life about him, and the power and clarity with which he wrote about so many important aspects of Welsh life and the human condition in general, these are the qualities which have impressed readers and writers of poetry much younger than himself. Prophetic and didactic in much of his work, Gwenallt was a central figure in the middle decades of this century.

A slightly younger contemporary of Gwenallt was Waldo Williams, who died in 1971, a poet whose output was small but whose every poem we treasure. The variety in his work stems from an impish sense of humour alternating with a profound, mystical, and therefore sometimes obscure view of the world immediately about him and of the universe that extends out from his loved background of Preseli. He was a pacifist and a Quaker, but it is for anyone who reads his poetry to judge whether his humanitarianism sprang from his religion or whether that was a formal pattern he accepted to crystallize his instinctive love of mankind in general. And Quakerism is surely the least formal religious pattern he could have found. Waldo Williams's thought is sometimes difficult to follow, but his language is always pure and near to the colloquial. In 'Cofio' (*Remembering*), he shows nostalgia for cultures, languages and faiths that have disappeared. Pembrokeshire is full of memorials of ways of living and thinking that are otherwise little known or understood today. Could he have been moved to fear that our culture and language may vanish just like those others that were once *lovely to the ear in the speech of little children (a thlws i'r clust ym mharabl plant bychain)*?

Waldo's patriotism and nationalism are of a kind we have seen too little of, for it has nothing of the swollen, false St David's Day rhetoric of memories of battles and blood favoured by our timorous, respectable society; rather is it based on a sensitive awareness of more peaceful qualities in the culture we have almost lost. . .

> *O Gymru'r gweundir gwrm a'i garn,*
> *Magwrfan annibyniaeth barn.*

(O Wales of the purple moorland and its cairn, / the place where independence of judgement was born.)

His poem 'Dewi Sant' (*St David*) comes nearest to anger when the poet contemplates the pollution that has come to south-west Pembrokeshire.

In spite of his gentle nostalgia for a more civilized way of living, Waldo Williams took a loving and hopeful view of the universe. In a poem called 'Yr Heniaith' (*The Old Language*) he has hopes of the survival of the Welsh language as well. Now that he is dead he appears to us not only as a great poet but as the conscience of Wales in our twentieth century.

I have been speaking of committed poets: the Reverend Euros Bowen (1904–88) stands apart in splendid luxuriance. I say apart not only because there is nothing didactic or propagandist in his poetry but because he belongs to no school, having, in the words of Dafydd Elis Thomas, developed a new poetic in Welsh. He is certainly not apart in the sense of not having paid attention to other writers; he read widely in French and English literature, he was a classical scholar who delightfully translated Virgil's eclogues into Welsh, and his poems display his debt to T. Gwynn Jones, Dafydd ap Gwilym and the poetic tradition from which he broke away. He has been thought obscure and has suffered eisteddfodic criticism on that account, but this is surely the impertinence of those who think that any poem should give up its secrets at first reading. Dafydd Elis Thomas (and how many countries have a member of parliament who is a sensitive critic of poetry?) has shown that the structure of a poem by Euros Bowen is not a logical progression (any more than was the 'Gododdin') but an interaction of images controlled by the imagination rather than the reason. Out of these images symbols grow which give the poem meanings which cannot be separated from the structure of the poem. His lack of general popularity may come from his being in many ways a poets' poet, and in fact a number of his poems are about poetry. Sometimes the poem is about the poem itself. 'Y Gerdd' (*The Poem*) is a remarkable twenty-line (*ugeined*) development of the idea of a poem as a place to live in. But his poems nearly always spring from a sense experience, and Euros Bowen's delight in the natural world is unfailing, giving the reader immediate pleasure even before the symbol begins to emerge.

'Golau' (*Light*), from his collection MYFYRION, an unusually long poem for Euros, is a review of the moods of Welsh poetry from its known beginnings, a beginning which the poet describes thus, in his own translation. . .

> Then a rising of light
> seizes the loins
> of the poet, and agitation
> of blood,
> seed of desire that would flower,
> young and ardent,
> a shoot
> nourishing a lust for the word
> still hidden
> morning and evening in the womb of the land.

In his own comments on this poem Euros Bowen says, *The poem comes to a close with an awareness that the poetic past is an illumination in the present.* So, however far back into the past a poem takes this poet, it never fails to illuminate the present. On his way to Troy he sees Turkish women harvesting in the fields, and having reached the ancient city he relates their captivity and long-suffering endurance to that of the Trojan women. On the same journey, before reaching the ruins, he is astonished to find something as familiar as blackberries ripening in this strange and distant landscape, and the berries become drops of blood on the brambles.

Completely untranslatable, even by the poet himself, and unique in Welsh writing, though not without its influence today, is the freedom of form into which Euros incorporates the devices of *cynghanedd*. The range of his vocabulary is immense, but, even so, when he feels it necessary he neologizes boldly. English readers may get some idea of his self-analysis and the magnificence of his delight in nature and in life from the poet's own translations of forty-four of his poems in POEMS (1974).

Until this present century Wales has enjoyed no continuous dramatic tradition, but over the past fifty years or so we have had a considerable flowering of this kind of writing; in the earlier years to feed amateur societies and chapel drama competitions, latterly to supply material for television and for the theatres which have sprung up, inspired and subsidized by the university colleges and other places of higher education, the regional associations of the Welsh Arts Council and the county education authorities, so that in Wales today one is never very far from a new, well-equipped if sometimes little theatre. Apart from Saunders Lewis our most interesting dramatist is Dr John Gwilym Jones, whose probings of our contemporary society have caught the attention of a widely ranging audience. An equally wide audience has been captured by the novels and short stories of Islwyn Ffowc Elis. Notable prose in specialist writing has come from J. R. Jones, the philosopher, R. T. Jenkins, historian, and Alwyn D. Rees, sociologist.

XVII

I draw the closing line beneath those great generations of Welsh writers who grew old with the century. Within the scope of this short book it would be invidious of me to select names from the very large number of interesting writers who are active today.

Suffice it to say that this is still a lively, varied and productive period in the history of Welsh writing.

Subsidies from the Welsh Arts Council and Welsh Books Council enable publishers to bring out books and magazines that would otherwise scarcely be viable for such a small market. But if the publisher is bolstered against loss, the author does not often make much money from his or her book. Yet the coming of a Welsh television channel has made it possible once again for a small number of writers to live by the pen.

Many of the new trends observable elsewhere apply in Welsh writing today, for example the emergence of feminist writing. But there is also continuity. A lively generation of young poets has taken up the craft of *cynghanedd*, and the National Eisteddfod continues to bring poets to the notice of a wide public. Eisteddfod poet, academic poet, 'bardd gwlad' (rural poet) and, more recently, urban poet, all flourish. If continuous tradition is strongest in poetry, then it is partly because of that living interplay, now as in the centuries which I have sought to describe, between a strong basis of versification and brilliant and bold modifications of the tradition.

For further reading

H. I. Bell, THE DEVELOPMENT OF WELSH POETRY, Oxford, 1936.

Rachel Bromwich, ASPECTS OF THE POETRY OF DAFYDD AP GWILYM, University of Wales Press, 1986

Rachel Bromwich, DAFYDD AP GWILYM: POEMS, Penguin Books, 1985.

Joseph P. Clancy, MEDIEVAL WELSH LYRICS, Macmillan, 1965.

Joseph P. Clancy, THE EARLIEST WELSH POETRY, Macmillan, 1970.

Anthony Conran, WELSH VERSE, Poetry Wales Press, 1986.

R. R. Davies, CONQUEST, COEXISTENCE AND CHANGE IN WALES 1063-1415, Oxford, 1987.

A. O. H. Jarman, Y GODODDIN, Gwasg Gomer, 1988.

Dafydd Jenkins, HYWEL DDA: THE LAW, Gwasg Gomer, 1986.

D. R. Johnston, GWAITH IOLO GOCH, Gwasg Prifysgol Cymru, 1988.

Gwyn Jones, THE OXFORD BOOK OF WELSH VERSE IN ENGLISH, Oxford, 1977.

Saunders Lewis, MEISTRI'R CANRIFOEDD, Gwasg Prifysgol Cymru, 1973.

Proinsias Mac Cana, THE MABINOGI, University of Wales Press, 1987.

Thomas Parry, A HISTORY OF WELSH LITERATURE, translated by H. I. Bell, Oxford, 1955.

Thomas Parry, HANES LLENYDDIAETH GYMRAEG HYD 1900, Gwasg Prifysgol Cymru, 1944.

Thomas Parry, THE OXFORD BOOK OF WELSH VERSE, Oxford, 1962.

Jenny Rowland, EARLY WELSH SAGA POETRY: A STUDY AND EDITION OF THE ENGLYNION, D. S. Brewer, 1990.

J. E. Caerwyn Williams, THE POETS OF THE WELSH PRINCES, University of Wales Press, 1978.

Glanmor Williams, RECOVERY, REORIENTATION AND REFORMATION: WALES c. 1415-1642, Oxford, 1987.

Gwyn Williams, THE BURNING TREE, Faber, 1956.

Gwyn Williams, TO LOOK FOR A WORD Gwasg Gomer, 1976.

Sir Ifor Williams, THE BEGINNINGS OF WELSH POETRY, edited by Rachel Bromwich, University of Wales Press, 1972.

The Author

GWYN WILLIAMS (1904–1990) was born in Port Talbot, of mixed Ceredigion and Vale of Glamorgan parentage. He was educated at Port Talbot County School, University College of Wales, Aberystwyth, and Jesus College, Oxford. Most of his working life was spent at universities of the Near East, Cairo, Alexandria, Benghazi and Istanbul, as lecturer and then professor of English Literature.

He published three volumes of verse, four novels, six volumes of translations from Welsh poetry, from THE RENT THAT'S DUE TO LOVE (Editions Poetry London, 1950) to TO LOOK FOR A WORD (Gwasg Gomer, 1976), works of criticism, including AN INTRODUCTION TO WELSH POETRY (Faber, 1953), books on Cyrenaica, Turkey and Wales, GREEN MOUNTAIN (Faber, 1963), TURKEY and EASTERN TURKEY (Faber, 1967 and 1972), TWRCI A'I PHOBL (Gwasg y Dref Wen, 1975), THE LAND REMEMBERS: A VIEW OF WALES (Faber, 1977). Three of his books have been re-issued in America and two of his recent books have been in Welsh. He was awarded the major Welsh Arts Council Literature Prize, 1977. In 1987 he published his COLLECTED POEMS 1936–1986.

Designed by Jeff Clements
Typesetting by BP Integraphics, Bath, in
11pt Palatino and printed in Great Britain by
Qualitex Printing Limited, Cardiff.

British Library Cataloguing in Publication Data

Williams, Gwyn, *1904-1990*
  An introduction to Welsh literature.-2nd ed
  (Writers of Wales)
  I. Title. II. Series
  891.6609

  ISBN 0-7083-1130-X

Published with the financial support of the Welsh Arts
Council